MARCO  POLO

OTTAWA

with **Local Tips**

The authors' special recommendations are highlighted in yellow throughout this guide

GW00702903

There are five symbols to help you find your way around this guide:

Marco Polo's top recommendations – the best in each category

sites with a scenic view

where the local people meet

where young people get together

(100/A1)
pages and coordinates for the street atlas
(O) outside area not covered by the city map

MARCO POLO

Travel guides and language guides in this series:

Alaska • Australia • Bahamas • Barbados • Berlin
Canada • Canada East • Canada West • California • Cuba
Dominican Republic • Florence • Florida • Ireland
London • Mexico • New York • Niagara Region • Paris • Prague
Rocky Mountains • Rome • San Francisco • Scotland • Tuscany
USA East • USA New England • USA Southern States • USA Southwest
Vancouver • Venice

*Marco Polo would be very interested to hear your
comments and suggestions. Please write to:*

*Marco Polo North America
70 Bloor Street East
Oshawa, Ontario, Canada • L1H 3M2
Tel. 905-436-2525
Web site: www.mapart.com*

*Our authors have done their research very carefully, but should any errors or omissions
have occurred, the publisher cannot be held responsible for any injury, damage
or inconvenience suffered due to incorrect information in this guide.*

*Cover photograph: Changing of the Guard, Parliament Hill (National Capital Commission)
Photos: Salvatore Sacco (7, 12, 19, 26, 31, 33, 34, 42, 44, 50, 52, 54, 58, 76, 82, 97); National Capital
Commission (5, 10, 17, 20, 22, 40, 60, 62, 70, 73, 74, 75, 94); Pierre St. Jacques (66)
Owl Rafting (38); Malak (64); Central Canada Exhibition (80)*

1st edition 2000
© MapArt Publishing Corporation Oshawa, Ontario/ Canada
Authors: Tracy Hanes & Betty VanHoogmoed
English edition: 2000 MapArt Corporation
Editorial director: Tracy Hanes
Associate editor: Betty VanHoogmoed
Cartography: Map Media Corporation, Oshawa, Ontario/Canada L1H 3M2
Design and layout: Thienhaus/Wippermann; Tracy Hanes
Printed in Canada

All rights reserved. No part of this publication may be reproduced or transmitted in any form or
by any means, electronic or mechanical, including photocopying, recording, or by any information storage
and retrieval systems without prior permission from the publisher.

CONTENTS

Discover Ottawa

*Canada's capital city abounds with
heritage buildings and natural beauty*

It seems difficult to imagine that this city of majestic boulevards, gracious parks, political power and a wealth of cultural riches got its start as a rough and tumble lumber town.

Today, it's the seat of government decision-making, the fourth largest municipality in Canada and home to some of the best educated, most affluent and most active citizens in the country. It has evolved into one of the world's most beautiful cities and a place where multiculturalism is embraced.

The city has been cited as one of the best places to live in Canada for its quality of life, clean air, fine public schools and libraries, affordable housing, good job prospects and cultural activities. Ottawa itself has 324,000 residents, while the National Capital Region, which

Ottawa is a cyclist's paradise, especially in spring when tulips bloom brilliantly along pathways and in parks.

includes Ottawa-Carleton on the Ontario side and Aylmer, Gatineau and Hull on the Quebec side, is home to 1.05 million people. Slightly more than half of the region's residents have English as a first language, while one-third speak French as well.

For visitors, there are numerous appeals: an abundance of parkland, stately Gothic buildings, a rich cultural scene, cosmopolitan cafes, specialty shops and many testaments to Canada's history.

Ottawa's centrepiece, and indeed the perfect place to kick off a visit, is Parliament Hill. Even visitors with little appetite for history and politics will be impressed by the grand spectre of the Parliament Buildings, set high above the Ottawa River. Their architecture, characterized by pointed arches, leaded glass windows, massive flying buttresses and gargoyles and grotesques, is simply stunning. And the changing of the guard, complete with brass band and marching men in red tunics and high black hats, is a true Canadian spectacle.

The eternal flame at the entrance to Parliament Hill was lit in 1967 to celebrate Canada's 100th birthday. The display of fire and water is fuelled by Alberta natural gas.

Equip yourself with a good pair of walking shoes and you can take in many major attractions without having to use a car. One of the city's main appeals is its compact core. Sites like Parliament Hill, the Supreme Court, Major's Hill Park, the Canadian Museum of Contemporary Photography, the Chateau Laurier, the National Gallery of Canada, the War Museum, the Royal Canadian Mint and the ByWard Market are in close proximity to one another.

Running through the centre of the city is the historic Rideau Canal, which winds 202 kilometres from Ottawa to Kingston. The system of natural lakes and rivers made navigable by locks, dams and canal cuts, was originally intended for defence and trading, but is primarily for pleasure now. The canal becomes the world's largest skating rink in winter, hosts a floating parade during May's annual Tulip Festival and is a busy route for boaters in summer.

The city is an architecture buff's dream, with heritage buildings co-existing with new landmarks like the National Gallery of Canada and the Canadian Museum of Civilization. (Because of the abundance of historic buildings, restoration is an ongoing project). A culture vulture risks overdose: there are 29 museums in the region, including 12 national institutions (most funded by taxpayers' dollars); and more than 50 galleries and theatres, including the National Arts Centre, and Arts Court, a centre for the visual and performing arts.

Monuments abound on Parliament Hill and in local parks. There are dozens of statues and monuments paying tribute to historical figures and events in Canadian and world history, from past prime ministers to peacekeepers to modern-day heroes like one-legged runner Terry Fox.

You might want to pack your bike or in-line skates (or ice skates in winter). So important is the pursuit of leisure in Ottawa that 170 kilometres of paved pathways, for cyclists and in-line skaters,

Brains and money

Ottawa has more university graduates than most Canadian cities. And they're better off financially too. In 1996, the average per capita income was about $24,000 per year, making Ottawa among the five highest ranking cities in Canada.

The Parliament Buildings as seen from across the river in Hull, Quebec

wind through the Capital Region. And every Sunday morning in summer, one of the city's parkways is closed to motorized traffic for Sunday Bike Days. In winter, the Rideau Canal becomes the world's longest skating rink and many residents don blades to commute to work. The tour from downtown along the Queen Elizabeth Parkway to Dows Lake, by foot, bike, in-line skates or car, is a great way to spend an afternoon; at the lake, you can partake of food and drink at the pavilion, rent pedal boats or canoes, or simply drink in the peaceful view from a park bench.

In spring the city is ablaze with colour, as millions of tulips bloom in park gardens. The initial 100,000 tulip bulbs were a gift from the Netherlands in gratitude for Canadian actions during World War II. Since then, the Netherlands has sent 10,000 bulbs a year and Canada buys more than 500,000 bulbs annually. Canada became the refuge for the Dutch Royal Family when it fled invading armies in 1940; and the heir to the throne, Princess Juliana, gave birth to daughter Margriet Francisca in Ottawa. Canadian troops also participated in the liberation of the

Netherlands and the tulips symbolize the lasting friendship between the two countries.

The plethora of parks and wilderness area around the city (the 'Emerald Necklace') is why it's called the Green Capital. Gatineau Park, an 85,440 acre wilderness conservation area is just minutes north of the city in Quebec; and the Greenbelt, a 42,240 acre protected band of farmland, wetland and forest rings the region, providing hiking, snowshoeing, cross country skiing and snowmobiling.

There is plenty too, for those who prefer less active pursuits. The city is blessed with an abundance of restaurants and bars, from fine dining establishments to casual fare to pubs. (The lively nightlife is partly due to the number of students in Ottawa and area: universities include the University of Ottawa, Carleton University and Université de Quebéc à Hull and colleges include Algonquin and La Cité Collegiale community colleges). For high rollers, world-class gambling can be had across the river in Hull at the Casino de Hull.

Commerce is an important aspect of the city's economy. From souvenirs to haute couture to Inuit art, Ottawa's got it, in indoor malls, historic shopping districts or colourful ethnic neighbourhoods.

For hundreds of years, trading has been a vital part of the city's history: Ottawa takes its name from the Indian word, Outaouak, the name of an Algonquin Indian tribe, which found the location at the juncture of the Rideau, Ottawa and Gatineau Rivers ideal for early trading activities.

French explorer Samuel de Champlain's arrival in the area in 1613 prompted an influx of Europeans eager to cash in on the lucrative fur-trading business, but they tended to settle in Montreal to the east.

The Ottawa area wasn't settled until 1800 when Philemon Wright and colonists from Massachusetts arrived on the north side of the river, below Chaudiere Falls, thus establishing Wright's Town (now Hull, Quebec). Wright launched the timber trade in the region and by 1830 the industry was booming.

The south side of the Ottawa River remained a wilderness until 1826 when Lieutenant Colonel John By of the Royal Engineers arrived to construct a navigable waterway, the Rideau Canal, between the Ottawa River and Kingston. He laid out a settlement, Bytown, for his men and built a bridge across to Chaudiere Falls.

The mammoth canal construction job brought a rich mix of cultures to the area: British military engineers, Scottish stone masons, Irish labourers, French-Canadian contractors and timber workers. The French and Irish settled mostly in Lowertown, while the Englishmen set up residence in Uppertown. Resentments festered between

History at a glance

1,500 years ago
First aboriginal people arrive after the last ice age, using Ottawa River as a transportation corridor.

1610
Étienne Brulé becomes the first European to explore the Ottawa River.

1613
French explorer Samuel de Champlain arrives and produces the first detailed maps of the area. He names fur-trading site Chaudière Falls (for "cauldron") and Rideau Falls.

1800
Philemon Wright and a group of colonists from Massachusetts settle in Wright's Town, on the north side of the river. It's now the City of Hull.

1806
Philemon Wright floats a timber raft down the Ottawa River to Quebec, proving logging in the area is feasible.

1826
The building of the Rideau Canal, under the supervision of Lt.-Col. John By, commences and continues until 1832. The settlement he lays out for his workers becomes Bytown.

1850s
American entrepreneurs open sawmills at Chaudière Falls, launching the boom in the Ottawa lumber industry.

1855
Bytown is incorporated as the City of Ottawa.

1857
Queen Victoria chooses Ottawa as capital of the United Provinces of Canada. The decision is widely criticized.

1866
The Parliament Buildings are completed after six years' construction, just in time for the arrival of Confederation a year later. They cost $4.5 million.

1892
Dr. James Naismith of Almonte, just west of Ottawa, invents the sport of basketball.

1900
The Great Fire starts in Hull at the lumber mills and crosses the river into Ottawa. Nearly 2,000 buildings are destroyed.

1916
The Centre Block burns to the ground on Capital Hill, leaving only the Library of Parliament standing.

1927
Prime Minister Mackenzie King makes the first international phone call to Britain's prime minister.

1945
Queen Juliana of the Netherlands presents Ottawa with 100,000 tulip bulbs.

Sculptors chisel works of art from ice during Winterlude celebrations.

Roman Catholic Lowertown and Protestant Uppertown, mainly because of living conditions. Lowertown was mostly wooden shanties, while Uppertown had several elegant mansions. Uppertown residents also administered the affairs of the town.

Racial tensions and political turmoil fostered violence in Bytown and the 1830s were marred by street fights, brawls, murders and assaults. An infamous day in Bytown history is Stoney Monday, when Lord Elgin, a Reformist-minded governor-general, announced he would pay a visit to Bytown. The Lowertowners wanted to welcome him; the Upper-towners wanted to ignore him. A riot erupted, where stones were thrown and one person shot dead. After that violent incident, the area became somewhat more peaceful.

Now, the ByWard Market (Lowertown) is one of the trendiest places to live, shop and eat in Ottawa. Until 30 years ago, it was the city's oldest blue-collar neighbourhood and the cradle of Ottawa's French population. Its history is one of fire, of farmers, of brawls and bawdiness. Now, it's packed with charming cafes, specialty shops, pubs and eateries of all descriptions and has a vibrant nightlife. (Elgin Street is another hot spot for night clubs).

The arrival of American entrepreneurs in the early 1850s changed the character of Ottawa once again. They built sawmills at Chaudiere Falls to satisfy the huge demand for sawn lumber in the U.S. and set the Ottawa Valley on its way to becoming the lumber capital of Canada.

The city's destiny changed forever when Queen Victoria named it as Canada's capital in

1857. The choice of the rough industrial town was controversial but there was method in the queen's madness: it was on the border of two provinces; the population was a mix of English and French-speaking inhabitants; it was easily reached by water and had publicly-held lands available for construction of government buildings.

The grand Parliament Buildings were completed in time for the birth of Confederation in 1867. They were modelled after Britain's House of Parliament but had to be almost completely rebuilt after a devastating fire in 1916 which left only the Parliamentary Library intact.

Still, the city was no jewel and when Wilfrid Laurier arrived in 1884, he lamented: "Ottawa is not a handsome city and does not appear destined to become one either." Once Laurier became prime minister, he played a key part in putting the polish on Ottawa by forming the Ottawa Improvement Commission in 1899 to beautify the city. And following World War II, at the invitation of Prime Minister Mackenzie King, French architect Jacques Gréber laid out the blueprint for the wide boulevards, scenic drives and generous green spaces that comprise the city today. His design is largely responsible for the Greenbelt, which includes a large, functioning farm within the city limits and Gatineau Park.

Because of its position as Canada's capital, Ottawa has enjoyed a stable economy and steady growth due to its government-related industries. But the economy is diversifying and the region has been dubbed 'Silicon Valley of the North' for its booming high tech field. One of the best known powerhouses is the Corel Corporation, headed by Michael Cowpland, whose socialite wife, Marlen, is a celebrity in her own right, thanks to her revealing fashions. More than 800 high tech companies are located in the Capital Region; Ottawa is also a leader in the health and life sciences field.

Ottawa is a city that knows how to celebrate with gusto, even when the mercury hits frigid temperatures. Winter, hot air balloons, tulips, music and Canada Day are all good reasons to throw a party in the nation's capital.

Swan song

In 1967, Queen Elizabeth II presented The Royal Swans to the city to commemorate her visit to the capital during Canada's Centennial year. The tradition continues annually as the swans glide along the Rideau River from May to November. One of the best places to view these graceful birds is Strathcona Park.

Exploring the city

There's no shortage of sightseeing delights,
from the Parliament Buildings to spectacular parks

One of the best ways to explore Ottawa is on foot. The city's compact core makes it ideal for walking and there are many major attractions, lovely parks, statues and monuments close at hand. It's easy to keep your bearings: landmarks like the Parliament Buildings, Chateau Laurier and National Gallery are easily visible from many downtown points. Don't jam-pack your schedule too tightly: the breath-taking National Gallery and its vast art collection is worth a half day visit or more, and don't rush your tour of the Parliament Buildings. After taking in the Changing of the Guard (daily summer mornings and evenings) and the official guided tour, pick up a self-guiding booklet and wander the grounds yourself. The river views are spectacular, so take your time.

The ByWard Market is prime for people-watching and for

Wellington Street, part of Confederation Blvd., is a good starting point for an Ottawa visit.

sipping a cold brew after a long day of sightseeing...again, just a short walk from downtown.

You will need wheels for sites such as the Agricultural Museum, the National Aviation Museum, the National Museum of Science and Technology and Rideau Hall. If you don't have a car, no problem: in addition to OC Transpo buses, the public transportation system, there are several operators with step-on, step-off tours. A short ride across the river to Hull, Quebec will take you to the Canadian Museum of Civilization, the Casino de Hull and the wild splendour of Gatineau Park.

Boat tours are another excellent way to enjoy the city's unique vantage point at the junction of three rivers, or take a bird's eye view of the region from a chartered plane.

ARCHITECTURE/MONUMENTS

There are numerous monuments and statues. Most downtown parks have at least one. Another prime spot is Parliament Hill, where you will find historic figures such as Queen Victoria, Lester B. Pearson, Sir George-Étienne Cartier, and Queen Elizabeth II immortalized in stone and bronze.

Canadian Museum of Civilization (100/J29)

〰️ This stunning architectural masterpiece showcases 1,000 years of human history. The building is a symbolic depiction of a land sculpted by wind, water and glaciers at the end of the Ice Age, when the first humans arrived in Canada from Asia.
100 Laurier St., Hull, Quebec; Tel. (819) 776-7000.

Canadian Tribute to Human Rights (104/L9)

The struggles of people around the globe to preserve fundamental human rights is honoured by this monument, commissioned and funded by a group of private citizens. The Dalai Lama, exiled religious and political leader of Tibet, unveiled the monument in 1990. It stands near the National War Memorial and was designed by Melvin Charney, a Montreal architect and artist. It serves as a gathering point for human rights demonstrations and speeches.
Corner of Elgin & Lisgar Streets

MARCO POLO SELECTION: SIGHTSEEING

1 Parliament Buildings
Pageantry, pomp, the politicians...and stunning Gothic architecture (page 20)

2 Rideau Canal
Historic canal is vital part of city life year-round (page 21)

3 ByWard Market
Eat, drink, shop or people watch (page 17)

4 Mackenzie King Estate
Gorgeous gardens, scenic ruins and more (page 19)

5 Commissioner's Park
Ablaze with tulips in May, pretty all year (page 24)

6 RCMP Stables
Meet the Mounties and their famous steeds (page 16)

7 National War Memorial
Striking centrepiece of Confederation Square (page 15)

8 Confederation Blvd.
Banner-decked route links major attractions (page 15)

9 Gatineau Park
Wilderness wonderland for hikers, bikers and nature lovers (page 24)

10 Major's Hill Park
City's oldest park with lovely views (page 25)

Confederation Blvd. (100/K30)

This route, which has won international awards for urban design, links many major attractions and national symbols. It circles through the heart of the Capital and joins the Ontario and Quebec sides of the Ottawa River. Along it, you'll find the Parliament Buildings, the Supreme Court of Canada, the Canadian Museum of Civilization, the National Gallery and several embassies. In warm weather months, it's a flag-decorated ceremonial route toured by foreign dignitaries. On Canada Day each year, it's closed to cars. During summer, banners remind passersby of important moments in the Canadian experience; while each winter, 45 landmarks along the boulevard are lit up by Christmas lights.

National War Memorial (100/K29)

This impressive memorial was designed to honour those who died in World War I, but wasn't unveiled until 1939 by King George VI — 20 years after the war ended. Now the 23 bronze figures emerging from a huge arch commemorate all of Canada's war dead. The annual National Remembrance ceremony is usually attended by many members of the public, the prime minister and Governor General. Confederation Square was designed with the memorial as its centrepiece, despite the traffic circulation problems it created.
Confederation Square, corner of Elgin and Wellington Streets.

Ottawa City Hall (100/J29)

While not as famous as the Parliament Buildings or the prime minister's house down the street, the seat of Ottawa municipal government is a beautiful structure. It features a dramatic addition by National Gallery of Canada architect Moshe Safdie. Tours available by appointment only.
111 Sussex Drive. Tel. (613) 244-5300; www.city.ottawa.on.ca.

Peacekeeping Monument (100/J29)

Three peacekeepers standing on walls above the debris of war, near a grove of young trees, honour the more than 80,000 Canadians who have served in the United Nations Peacekeeping Forces since 1948. The memorial was designed by sculptor Jack Harman, urban designer Richard Henriquez and landscape architect Cornelia Oberlander.
Sussex Drive and St. Patrick Street.

Terry Fox Statue (100/K29)

Canada's legendary runner Terry Fox, who lost a leg to cancer, is immortalized in this statue by John Hooper. The Vancouver youth's coast-to-coast 'Marathon of Hope' to raise money for cancer research started in April 1980 in Newfoundland but ended when he collapsed outside of Thunder Bay, Ontario on September 1 the same year. Although Fox did not complete his run and died a year later, he raised $25 million for cancer research. His legacy lives on in public buildings, a stamp and an annual nation-wide run.

In front of Parliament Hill, corner of Metcalfe and Wellington St.

CULTURE

Canada & the World Pavilion (100/J30)

〰️ This pavilion, set to open in late summer 2000, pays homage to the numerous internationally recognized achievements by Canadians. Stunning vistas of Ottawa and Rideau Rivers.

Rideau Falls Park, Sussex Drive.

Carleton University Art Gallery (103/P27)

Ottawa's big little art gallery features changing exhibitions of Canadian and international painting, sculpture, drawing, print-making and photography. Inuit art is always on view.

Closed Mon. Sept.-May: Tues.-Fri. Noon-7pm. Sat. & Sun. Noon-5pm. June-Aug.: Tues.-Sun. Noon-6pm. Free admission. 1125 Colonel By Drive, St. Patrick's Building. Tel. (613) 520-2120.

Le Cordon Bleu Ottawa Culinary Institute (103/P26)

French cuisine and pastry are on the menu at this internationally based culinary arts school. Demonstration classes open to the public. Specialty courses and short programs for personal interest.

400-1390 Prince of Wales Drive; Tel. (613) 224-8603; www.cordonbleu.net.

Corel Centre (0)

Dubbed the "coolest arena on earth," this 18,500 seat sports and entertainment facility is home of the Ottawa Senators NHL team.

1000 Palladium Drive, Kanata; Tel. (613) 599-0250; www.corelcentre.com

RCMP Stables (101/K32)

One of the most beloved symbols of Canada are the red-coated Mounties astride black horses. And the famed Royal Canadian Mounted Police's Musical Ride has been thrilling global audiences for more than a century. The Musical Ride team is usually on tour from June to September, during other months you can catch the Mounties putting their horses through their paces in the arena. (Other RCMP horses are stabled there during summer). Guided half-hour tours.

Sept.-Apr.: Mon.-Fri. 8:30am-3pm. Closed Sat. & Sun. May-Aug.: Mon.-Fri.: 8:30am-4pm. Sat. & Sun.: 10am-4pm. Free admission. St. Laurent Blvd. and Sandridge Rd.; Tel. (613) 993-3751.

Turtle Island Tourism Co. (100/K28)

Hear Inuit throat singers, feel the pulse of pounding drums and enjoy the colourful spectacle of First Nations dancers in full regalia. This First Nations experience also offers traditional foods, crafts and storytelling on Victoria Island, a historic meeting place for aboriginal people of the area. Interactive demonstrations; meals by an award-winning chef. Souvenirs and crafts for sale too. Custom tours available. 10am-8pm May-Oct. Trading Post open daily 9am-9pm.

National War Memorial

was the scene of one of the worst breakdowns in public order when the "Stoney Monday" riot caused one death and many injuries. The ruckus was between supporters of two political parties who argued with fists, stones, vegetables and firearms over the visit of the Governor General. The many 19th century buildings lend a historic ambience and at the edge of the market is the Cathedral-Basilica of Notre Dame, which features more than 200 statues.

The market is bordered by Sussex Drive, St. Patrick, King Edward and Rideau Streets.

Victoria Island (behind Parliament Hill between Ottawa and Hull). Tel. (613) 564-9494 or 1-877-811-3233.

MARKETS

ByWard Market   (100/K29)

★ ✿ ⚘ This colourful mosaic of farmers' market stalls, galleries, shops, cafes and clubs just east of Parliament Hill has been an open air market since the 1840s. Today this bustling area is chockful of restaurants serving food from around the world, specialty shops with arts, crafts and other unique products, and fresh farm produce.

It's worth a stroll through the market, even if you don't plan to spend a penny. On the Mile of History on Sussex Drive, upscale stores are housed in beautiful stone buildings and outdoor cafes are plentiful in cobblestone courtyards. In 1849, the market

Ottawa Antique Market   (104/L29)

★ Fifty independent antique and collectible dealers gather daily year-round 10 minutes from Parliament Hill. Exceptional collection of china, antiques, collectibles, Art Deco, jewellery, country furniture and much more. *Open 10am-6pm every day. 1179 Bank Street; (613) 730-6000.*

Somerset Heights   (104/L28)

Get a glimpse into the Far East in this downtown Asian village marketplace. Find one-of-a-kind treasures in every nook, from rice noodles to painted silk, or bargain for delicacies like chicken's feet. *Somerset Street West from Bay to Rochester.*

Sparks Street Mall   (100/K29)

✿ Canada's first pedestrian-only mall was created in 1961 by the merchants of Sparks Street, thus barring motorized traffic from the street. Shops and services line the historic street and there are special events year-round and an outdoor market in summer. *Sparks Street, between Elgin and Lyon Streets.*

POLITICS & HISTORY

Arts Court (100/K29)
★ ❂ This 1871 heritage building is home to more than 20 local arts organizations, two visual art galleries and a 120-seat studio theatre. The Ottawa Art Gallery showcases local and Canadian artists; Le Groupe de la Place Royal Dance Lab is the only lab dedicated to dance research and development; and the Carleton University Art Gallery has a small but representational collection of Canadian and European Art. *Galleries open Tues.-Wed. 10am-5pm. Thurs. 10am-5pm, Fri. 10am-5pm, Sat. & Sun. Noon-5pm; 2 Daly Ave.; Tel. (613) 564-7240.*

Beechwood Cemetery (101/K32)
One of the country's most historic cemeteries. Buried here are Sir Robert Borden, prime minister from 1911 to 1920; Sir Sandford Fleming, who invented Standard Time; pulp, paper and railway baron John Boothe, to name a few. Annual guided tour of the grounds or do-it-yourself. There's also a historical site. *Open year round, Mon. to Fri.: 8am-5pm; Sat. 8am-4pm; Sun. 9am-4pm. 280 Beechwood Ave. Tel. (613) 741-9530.*

Cartier Square Drill Hall (101/K30)
Every morning during summer, the Governor General's Foot Guard assembles here to march to Parliament Hill for the Changing of the Guard. Arrive at 9:30am to follow the marchers along their parade route. Small regimental museum, with displays of uniforms, weapons and photos. *Laurier Ave. beside Queen Elizabeth Driveway.*

Laurier House National Historic Site (101/K31)
Two prominent Canadian prime ministers – Sir Wilfrid Laurier and William Lyon Mackenzie King – called this stately residence home. While several rooms are devoted to Laurier's mementos and furnishings, the majority of the house evokes the King era of the 1920s and '30s, filled with memorabilia and gifts from around the world. King's

---

The fierce faces of Parliament

Those intense faces on the Peace Tower belong to gargoyles and grotesques. Resembling animals, people or creatures, these figures were carved into stone to enhance the building's neo-Gothic look. Gargoyles' roots are spiritual and practical. They were originally created to ward off evil and to drain rainwater away from the building. A project is currently in the works to determine the historical chronicle of every carving. As for the intense faces you see inside Parliament, those are Canada's decision makers, the Members of Parliament.

The Changing of the Guard, daily during summer, is a Canadian spectacle.

third floor study contains the crystal ball he used to seek spirits' help in decision-making.

Sept.-Apr.: Closed Mon.; Tues.-Sat. 10am-5pm, Sun. 2pm-5pm. May-Aug.: Mon. Noon-8pm, Tues.-Sat. 9am-5pm, Sun. 2pm-5pm. Adults $2.25; Seniors $1.75; Students $1.25; Kids under 6: Free admission. 335 Laurier Avenue East; Tel. (613) 992-8142.

Mackenzie King Estate (99/G26)

🔆 ★ Canada's longest-serving prime minister was more than a brilliant politician. William Lyon Mackenzie King also loved nature and was an avid amateur architect, reflected in his estate in Gatineau Park. He built Kingswood, a small one bedroom cottage in 1903, moved to a larger cottage, Moorside in 1928, and in the later 1930s, relocated to a larger, winterized home, The Farm. His picturesque ruins, carefully-designed flower beds and lawns remain as a testament to his love of the land.

Mid-May to mid-Oct.: Mon.-Fri. 11am-5pm; Sat. & Sun. 10am-6 pm. Admission $6 per car or $20 per minibus. Gatineau Park; Tel. (819) 827-2020.

Ottawa International Hostel (100/K30)

This heritage building, which now provides budget accommodation, is rich in history. Formerly the Carleton County Jail from 1862 to 1972, it was the site of the last public hanging in Canada in the 1960s. Guided tours will thrill the morbidly curious with a look at the gallows, prisoners' cells, death row and the public stocks. Guides also explain the jail's history and describe prison conditions of the past.

Tours $3 per person. (Call ahead for times) 75 Nicholas St. Tel. (613) 235-2595.

The picturesque ruins at Mackenzie King Estate in Gatineau Park.

Ottawa Locks   (100/K29)

This picturesque ladder of eight gates between the Ottawa River and the Chateau Laurier is a good way to spend a sunny afternoon, watching pleasure craft ply the canal. Like most locks on the Rideau Canal, these are still opened and closed manually behind boats moving upstream.
Behind Chateau Laurier.

Parliament Buildings   (100/K29)

★ With a commanding setting on the cliffs above the Ottawa River and a stately stone exterior, this national symbol of power has been described as one of the most beautiful government centres on the globe. The Neo-Gothic buildings contain the House of Commons, the Library of Parliament, the Hall of Honour, the Senate and the majestic Peace Tower. The Changing of the Guard, daily at 10am on the Hill from late June to late August, weather permitting, is a true Canadian spectacle. In summer, start at the Info-Tent, a large white tent between the Centre and West Blocks, where you can get same-day tickets for all tours, pick up an outdoor self-guiding booklet or talk to interpretive staff. In non-summer months, go to the Visitor Welcome Centre in the Centre Block. Centre Block Tours are offered daily except New Year's, Canada Day and Christmas. Also, don't miss the view from the Peace Tower's observation deck. The East Block, the pulse of Canadian government for the first 100 years, features four restored Confederation-era rooms. (Tickets required). To see federal politicians in action, you can obtain passes to sit in the public galleries of the Senate and House of Commons. For a retrospective of the nation's history, an outdoor guided tour takes visitors to the statues of former prime ministers to explain how they've shaped Canada's past, present and future. *Sept.-May: 9am-4pm every day. Open 'til 8pm on Tues. 'til early Oct. June-Aug.: Mon.-Fri. 9am-8pm. Weekends & holidays: 9am-5pm. Parliament Hill; Tel. (613) 992-4793 or (613) 239-5000.*

Here are some of the sights to take in during a tour of the Hill:
Centre Block
This is the most recognizable of the buildings on Parliament Hill, home to the House of Commons, the Senate and the Library of Parliament. It was rebuilt in 1916 after being destroyed by fire.
East Block
Canada's first prime minister, Sir John A. Macdonald, had offices in this block. The 1867 section is built in the Victorian Gothic style with turrets, arches and wrought iron details. The less elaborate 1910 segment was built to provide government staff offices and security for valuables. The 1910 section now features four rooms which have been restored to reflect the era of Confederation (1867).
Peace Tower
The 92.2 metre structure re-opened in 1996 after undergoing $9.9 million in renovations to stop its deterioration. There are 25,000 stones in the tower — including Nepean, Ohio and Wallace

sandstones and granites — and 53 bells in the Carillon. Enjoy the view from the observation deck.

Prime Minister's Residence   (101/H31)
You can barely glimpse the stone mansion at 24 Sussex Drive behind the dense foliage, but this place has been home to Canadian prime ministers since 1943 when the government bought it. It's not open to the public, but you can peek from the street.
24 Sussex Drive.

Rideau Canal   (104/M29)
❁ ★ This historic canal is an integral part of the city's vibrant spirit. The eight-kilometre Canal Promenade runs from downtown along Colonel By Drive to the Hartwell Locks at Carleton University. Tulips bloom along its parkways in May; cyclists, joggers and picnickers are out in force in the summer; and in winter, it's the world's longest skating rink and the site of Winterlude.

Rideau Hall   (101/J31)
The official residence of the Governor General is open for tours of its principal rooms and spectacular gardens. Start at the Visitor Centre with its interactive exhibit and gift shop. Guides dressed in period costumes roam the house and grounds and there are horticultural tours, children's activities, outdoor concerts, etc. *Sept.-May: Sat. & Sun. Noon-4pm. May-June: Sat. & Sun. 10am-4pm. July-Aug. 10am-4pm daily. Visitor Centre open daily 9:30am-5:30pm.*

The historic Rideau Canal is a focal point for vibrant Ottawa life.

Free admission. 1 Sussex Drive. Tel. (613) 998-7113.

Royal Canadian Mint (100/J29)

Marvel at $1 million worth of gold bullion on display here or learn how coins are made. Find an addition for your coin collection, a unique gift or a souvenir at the boutique.
Reservations necessary for tours. Sept.-May: Tours offered daily. May-Aug. Mon.-Wed. 9am-5pm; Thurs.-Fri. 9am-7pm, Sat. & Sun. 9am-4pm. Admission $2 per person. Family $8. 320 Sussex Drive. Tel. (613) 993-8990.

St. Patrick's Basilica (104/L28)

The oldest parish in Ottawa to serve English-speaking Catholics was completed in 1875 and features a modern Gothic design inside, enhanced by sacred paintings, stained glass windows, pipe organ, marble altars and statues.
281 Nepean at Kent Street; Tel. (613) 233-1125.

Supreme Court of Canada (100/K28)

Fittingly, this stately hall of justice makes a boldly impressive statement a mere two minute walk west of the Parliament Buildings. The 1946 court is topped with the green copper roofing that has become a colourful symbol of the nation's capital. *Sept.-Apr.: Guided tours by reservation. Mon.-Fri. 9am-5pm, May-Aug.: No reservations needed. 9am-5pm daily. Free admission. Kent and Wellington Streets; Tel. (613) 995-4330 or (613) 995-5361.*

Watson's Mill (0)

The 1860 mill has its very own ghost: according to legend, the wife of the mill owner fell into the grinding machine and died. Allegedly, her spirit still haunts. The mill is completely restored and functional and guides tell about its history. A farmers' market is held Saturday mornings May to October.

5525 Dickinson Street, Manotick (East on Rte. 13, about 30 minutes from Capital Hill); Tel. (613) 692-2500.

NEIGHBOURHOODS

ByWard Market & Lowertown (100/K29)

❀ This oldest section of the city, north-east of the Parliament Buildings, is best known for the ByWard Market, Canada's oldest farmers' market and home to 350 specialty shops, eateries and services. Once a cedar swamp land, Lowertown, where Ottawa's first labourers settled, gained a reputation as a dangerous and rowdy area until the 1850s. Today, it's a showcase for French Canadian architecture and quaint shops. It's also one of the trendiest places to live, shop and go out. The courtyards, which are interior pedestrian spaces, were once used to store junk and dispose of garbage. The most popular courtyard is Tin House Court, named for a house that belonged to a blacksmith. The house was demolished during urban renewal, but its facade hangs on the wall. Another notable site is the now faded hotel, Chateau Lafayette, on York Street. Built in 1849, it played host to Queen Victoria. Clarendon Court, on the corner of George and Sussex, was originally a log tavern.

(See location under Markets in this chapter)

Glebe (104/N29)

The city's first suburb boasts charming old houses, extensive parks and tree-lined streets, as well as specialty shops, restaurants and pubs.

Along Bank Street from the Queensway to Lansdowne Park.

Little Italy (103/M27)

Also known as Corso Italy in tribute to its proud heritage. Vibrant area of fine restaurants, gift stores and pasticcerias. This community pulses with energy during the annual Italian Week Festival in June.

Preston Street, north of Dows Lake.

Somerset Heights (104/L28)

Bustling multicultural business area featuring food and goods from around the world. Home to Chinatown, where there are dozens of Chinese, Thai and Vietnamese restaurants and markets selling Asian produce, crafts, potions, herbs, etc. It's worth a visit to soak up the atmosphere.

(See location under Markets)

Somerset Village (104/L29)

This heritage district was one of Ottawa's first commercial areas. The one-block district has restaurants and specialty shops.

Between Bank and O'Connor Streets.

Sussex Drive (101/J30)

One of the grandest boulevards in Canada. Some of the nation's best-known landmarks, such as the National Gallery of Canada, the Royal Canadian Mint, the Canadian War Museum and Notre Dame Basilica are located here. So are the prime minister and Governor General's homes, Rideau Falls, Ottawa City Hall, the Lester B. Pearson Building and the French embassy.

Westboro Village (98/K23)

Originally a small village on the outskirts, this neighbourhood has an eclectic mix of shops, services and restaurants, a small town flavour and 'Elvis Lives Lane.'
West after Wellington Street becomes Richmond Road.

PARKS AND GARDENS

Andrew Haydon Park (0)

Lovely river views are offered, as well as a picnic site, food concessions, washrooms and small artificial lake. Swimming's not recommended. Home of the Nepean Sailing Club.
Acres Road and Carling Avenue.

Commissioners Park (104/L29)

More than 300,000 tulips bloom in spectacular living colour in this beautiful park at Dows Lake near the Rideau Canal, making it a shutterbug's paradise. Annual plants bloom during summer.
Queen Elizabeth Parkway.

Confederation Park (104/L29)

Site of many major events, including Winterlude and the Ottawa International Jazz Festival. The fountain once stood in Trafalgar Square in London, England.
Elgin Street and Laurier Avenue.

Dows Lake (103/N27)

★ ♨ ❀ This favourite gathering place for picnickers and nature lovers was created during construction of the Rideau Canal. It's surrounded by picturesque pathways and is close to the Central Experimental Farm. Choose from two restaurants and a cafe in the Dows Lake Pavilion. Rent canoes and pedal boats in summer; skates and sleighs in winter.
Queen Elizabeth Parkway.

Garden of the Provinces (100/K28)

The union of Canada's provinces and territories is commemorated with two symbolic fountains and a display of all the provinces' arms and floral emblems.
Wellington Street at Bay Street.

Gatineau Park (99/G26)

★ ♨ ❀ More than a million people flock here each summer to walk, cycle, mountain bike, in-line skate, swim, camp, canoe, ski or simply relax. The park, minutes from downtown, covers 35,000 hectares of the Canadian Shield in western Quebec and is habitat to deer, wolf, bear, beaver and numerous plant species. Explore green spaces, clear lakes, forests and panoramic vistas on 125 kilometres of mountain bike and hiking trails. Also the site of the Mackenzie King Estate, home of Canada's longest serving prime minister. The Gatineau Park Visitor Centre is open year-round.

Cross the Macdonald-Cartier Bridge, which becomes Highway 5. Take Exit 12 (Chelsea, Gatineau Park), turn left on Old Chelsea Road; continue straight on Meech Lake Road to #318.

Hog's Back Falls (103/P26)

This popular picnic spot at the point where the Rideau Canal meets the Rideau River is named for the rocks that resemble bristles on a hog's back.

Colonel By Drive to Hog's Back Bridge.

Jacques Cartier Park (100/J29)

One of the best views of the Rideau Falls and city skyline can be had from this spot on the Ottawa River in Hull. Popular haven for walkers and cyclists. The Maison du Velo is a resource for bike riders.

Between Alexandra and Macdonald-Cartier bridges.

Leamy Lake Ecological Park and Archaeological Site (0)

Rich bird life and lush vegetation are in abundance; the park also offers windsurfing and many amenities. Watch archaeologists in action or talk to an interpretive staff member to learn about the ancient history and recent artifact discoveries.

Head east along Highway 148 to Leamy Lake Parkway, Hull.

Major's Hill Park (100/K29)

The city's oldest park, dating back to 1874, affords stunning views of the Ottawa River, Hull, Parliament Buildings, and the Rideau Canal. Site of craft fairs and concerts in summer. At the section behind the National Gallery of Canada is the Astrolabe Theatre.

Mackenzie Avenue behind the Chateau Laurier.

Mer Bleue Conservation Area (0)

You'll swear you're in a northern landscape after visiting the vast peat bog, complete with interpretive trail, at this unique ecological site on the southeastern edge of the city. Rare southern example of boreal forest, where stunted tamarack and black spruce trees grow. Seven trails offer 20 kilometres of hiking and cross country skiing.

Follow Innes Road to Anderson Road, then south to Borthwick Road and follow the signs.

New Edinburgh Park (101/J30)

Peaceful natural park on the eastern bank of the Rideau River with plenty of wildlife, including blue herons, muskrats, turtles, butterflies and more. Skate on an outdoor rink in winter.

Corner of Stanley Ave. and Dufferin Rd.

Rideau Falls Park (101/J30)

This charming small park, opposite City Hall, offers a mighty view of Rideau Falls, plus

Major's Hill Park is Ottawa's oldest park and offers stunning views.

walking paths and well-tended gardens.
Sussex Drive at Stanley Avenue.

Rockcliffe Park (100/J31)

❧ Another great place to picnic, complete with stone shelter and the Rockeries, lovely gardens which bloom grandly from spring to fall. A wooded urban oasis set in the upscale Rockcliffe Park neighbourhood, where many ambassadors live. *Rockcliffe Parkway at Princess Avenue.*

Stony Swamp Conservation Area (0)

Wildlife abounds in the fields, forests and ponds in the west Greenbelt region. A 38-kilometre trail network – for hiking, skiing or snowshoeing – includes the Kingston to Ottawa Rideau Trail. *Moodie Drive and Knoxdale Road.*

Strathcona Park (105/L31)

Let the kids splash in the wading pool or frolic in the playground while you relax on a bench under huge trees and watch the Royal Swans glide by on the Rideau River. The Odyssey Theatre performs in summer in this park in the Sandy Hill area east of Laurier House. Unique features include the concrete castle ruins with statues of rabbits, pigs and other animals. *Range Road and Laurier Avenue East.*

Trans Canada Trail (100/K29)

This national treasure winds through the Capital Region from Stittsville in the west through the Greenbelt to the Ottawa River Recreation Path and crosses the Rideau Canal downtown. It continues across the Alexandra Bridge to Hull, Quebec and on.

Trans Canada Trail Pavilions stand at Jacques Cartier Park and between the Portage Bridge and Commissioner Bridge.

Vincent Massey Park (103/P27)

❧ This lovely park near Hog's Back Falls can accommodate a crowd, with hundreds of picnic tables and fireplaces; sports fields and recreation paths too. And across the road at Mooney's Bay, you'll find a marina and beach.

Heron Road west of Riverside Drive.

TOURS

Air

Air Outaouais
Seaplane sightseeing tours over Meech Lake, Gatineau Park, etc. take-off from the Ottawa River. $35-$460. Tel.: (819) 568-2359.

High Time Balloon Co.
Hot air balloon adventure over Ottawa. With champagne.
$125 per passenger. Tel. (613) 521-9921.

Boat

Ottawa Riverboat Co. Ltd.
Six daily excursions, weekly dining, special events, charters

on elegant double-decker ships. Full day excursions to Chateau Montebello. Tel.: (613) 562-4888.

Paul's Boat Lines Ltd.
Cruises on the Rideau Canal (*$12*) or Ottawa River (*$14*). Bilingual commentary. Kiosk on Wellington near Parliament Hill. Tel.: (613) 225-6781.

St. Lawrence Cruise Lines
Four, five or six night riverboat cruises on the St. Lawrence and Ottawa rivers. Ottawa, Kingston, Montreal and Quebec City departures. $1,027 -$1,999. Tel.: (613) 549-8091 or 1-800-267-7868.

Bus

Capital Double Decker Tours
Rated the city's best sightseeing tour. Bilingual with 15 stops on double decker buses. You can get on and off as you please. Tickets (*$17*) valid for two days, free hotel pick-up. Evening tours in July & August. Kiosk at Sparks and Metcalfe Streets; Tel: (613) 749-3666 or 1-800-823-6147.

On Foot

Parliament Hill
Centre Block Tours include the House of Commons and Senate in a 45-minute guided tour. Tickets at Info-Tent during summer and Visitor Welcome Centre other times of the year.

The Haunted Walk of Ottawa
Light up the lantern and listen to Ottawa ghost stories in this unusual walking tour. 90 minute tours seven days a week; $8. 7 & 9pm from D'Arcy McGee's Pub, Sparks & Elgin Streets; Tel. (613) 730-0575; www.hauntedwalk.com

Steeped in history

*Civilization, aviation, science and photography
are well represented at Ottawa's many museums*

When it comes to cultural institutions, Ottawa has the motherlode, boasting 29 museums in the region. A dozen of those are national institutions, financed mainly by taxpayers' dollars. Whether it's planes, farm animals, coins, science or civilization, you'll find a museum devoted to a diverse range of interests.

Agricultural Museum (103/N26)

See farm animals up close at this unique museum in the heart of the Capital, on the 500-hectare Central Experimental Farm. This government research station includes: a barn containing 1920s' artifacts; herds of cows, cattle, pigs, sheep, horses, chickens and rabbits; a modern dairy operation; and exhibits, such as one which tells the story of where the bread on our table comes from. Special events and seasonal hands-on activities

The Great Hall in the Canadian Museum of Civilization celebrates aboriginal culture.

include sheep shearing, cow milking and goat leading. Ornamental gardens and an arboretum with more than 2,000 varieties of trees and shrubs grace the landscape.
9am-5pm daily except Christmas; Admission: Adults $3; seniors $2; children (3-15 years) and students $2. Children under 3: free. Experimental Farm Drive; Tel. (613) 991-3044.

Bank of Canada's Currency Museum (100/K29)

Fascinating look at the evolution of money around the globe and through the ages. Mediums of exchange include shells, teeth, cocoa beans and modern-day coins and bills. On display in the garden court is the Yap stone, from the island of Yap. Stones shaped like this one – more than two meters in diameter and weighing three tons – were used as money up to modern times on the South Pacific island.
May-Sept.: Sun. 1pm-5pm; Mon.-Sat. 10:30am-5pm; Sept.-Apr.: Sun. 1pm-5pm. Tues.-Sat. 10:30am-5pm, closed Mon. Admission: free. 245 Sparks Street; Tel. (613) 782-8914.

MARCO POLO SELECTION: MUSEUMS

1 Canadian Museum of Civilization
1,000 years of human history are chronicled in fascinating fashion (page 31)

2 National Gallery of Canada
The country's finest collection of Canadian and European art in a glass and granite masterpiece (page 36)

3 National Museum of Science and Technology
Science class was never this much fun (page 37)

4 Agricultural Museum
The animals on this modern working farm in a heritage setting bring our rural roots to life (page 29)

5 Canadian War Museum
Revel in heroic tales and examine the human cost of war (page 33)

6 Canadian Museum of Contemporary Photography
The talents of this country's top photographers are showcased (page 32)

Billings Estate Museum   (100/K29)

The treasures of four generations of one of the city's founding families are on display in this 1829 house, a national historic site.
May-Oct.: Tues.-Sun. noon to 5pm; Adults $2.50; seniors $2; children and students $1.50. 2100 Cabot Street; Tel. (613) 247-4830.

Bytown Museum   (104/L29)

The history of Bytown is chronicled in this 1827 building, the oldest stone structure in Ottawa, originally a treasury for the payroll of the men building the Rideau Canal and a storehouse for their equipment. Admission to the canal-builders exhibit, which includes photographs, posters and mannequins, is free. In other parts of the museum, which you must pay to see, a display honours Lieu-

tenant-Colonel John By, the canal's chief engineer, and there are re-creations of a pioneer kitchen, Victorian parlour and lumber-man's shanty. The antique toy store has porcelain dolls, toy soldiers and other playthings.
Apr.-May & Oct.-Nov.: Mon.-Fri., 10am-4pm; May-Oct.: Mon.-Sat.: 10am-5pm; Sun. 1-5pm; Dec.-Mar.: 8am-4pm or by appointment. Admission: Adults $2.50; seniors $2; children and students $1.50. Beside Ottawa Locks near Chateau Laurier. Tel. (613) 234-4570.

Canadian Children's Museum   (104/L29)

On site at the Canadian Museum of Civilization, reputedly one of the largest children's museums in the world. Youngsters can embark on a Great Adventure trip around the world and enjoy the kid-sized, hands-on, interactive exhibits. They can also visit a pyramid with a secret passage, make Mexican tortillas, steer a freighter or walk through a rain forest. Computer games, arts and crafts and storytellers too. Open to kids up to 14.

May-mid. Oct.: 9am-6pm; until 9pm Thurs. & Fri. Mid-Oct.-Apr.: 9am-5pm; closed Mon. Adults $8; seniors $7; youth $6, kids under 12 $3, families $18. Sun. admission is free from 9am-noon. 100 Laurier St., Hull. Tel. (819) 776-8294.

Canadian Museum of Civilization (104/L29)

★ ☙ This architectural marvel boasts an impressive view of the Parliament Buildings and illustrates more than 10,000 years of Canadian pre-history, history and culture. Give yourself a full day or more to take it all in. Three major galleries present permanent collections where sound, images and treasures trace Canada's development: the soaring Grand Hall celebrates aboriginal culture from the Pacific Northwest Coast with massive totem poles, cedar plank houses and artifacts from six different coastal nations; the Canada Hall uses large-scale settings to portray key periods in history, from the arrival of Norse explorers in Canada up to the settlement of western Canada; the First People's Hall celebrates the diversity of our longest-established cultures. Temporary

Ceiling in the Great Hall of the Canadian Museum of Civilization.

exhibitions showcase subjects such as archaeology, history, folk culture and ethnology. The world's first combined Imax Omnimax theatre takes you on an amazing sensory adventure like you've never experienced. Also on site is the Canadian Children's Museum and the Canadian Postal Museum. Outdoors, enjoy one of the most breath-taking views the area has to offer.

April-mid Oct.: daily 9am-6pm; Thurs. & Fri. to 9pm. Mid-Oct.-late Mar.: Tues.-Sun. 9am-5pm: Thurs. to 9pm. Admission varies depending on season, age, etc. 100 Laurier St., Hull, Quebec; Tel. (819) 776-7000 or 1-800-555-5621; www.civilization.ca.

Canadian Museum of Contemporary Photography (100/K29)

★ The talents of the country's most creative photographers are celebrated in this converted railway tunnel overlooking the Rideau Canal. More than 159,000 photographs in the collection are guaranteed to shock, excite or move visitors. Exhibits change every few months. Meet the artists, attend workshops or buy a photographic treasure in the boutique.

May-Sept.: Mon., Tues., Fri., Sat. & Sun. 11am-5pm; Wed. 4-8pm, Thurs. 11am-8pm. Sept.-Apr.: Wed., Fri., Sat. & Sun. 11am-5pm. Thurs., 11am-8pm. Closed Mon. & Tues. Admission by donation. 1 Rideau Canal; Tel. (613) 990-8257.

Canadian Museum of Nature (104/L29)

This kid-friendly museum displays natural history at its best, in the form of five million specimens from dinosaurs to precious gems. Seven signature galleries are as varied as Mother Nature herself: experience the depths of a gold mine or learn about Arctic polar bears. Get right up close to stuffed mammals and birds, and spy on live creepy crawlers. Audio visual shows, lectures and children's discovery area. Home to the Viola MacMillan Mineral Gallery with its marvellous mineral displays.

May-Sept.: daily 9:30am-5pm. (Thurs. to 8pm); Sept.-Apr.: Tues.-Sun., 10am-5pm, Thurs. to 8pm. Adults $5; seniors/students $4; children (3-12) $2; families $12. 240 McLeod St.; Tel. (613) 566-4700; www.nature.ca.

Canadian Postal Museum (100/J29)

Even the mail can make for

Street of Gold

Thar's gold in them thar... sewers? If there's an unexplained spring in your step as you walk along Wellington, it's because the world's largest single gold depository is right underneath your feet. The Bank of Canada's gold vaults are located underground. Now that's cold hard cash.

Military history comes alive at the Canadian War Museum on Sussex Drive.

fascinating fodder. See a multitude of postal curiosities, from the first Canadian stamp to the high-tech machinery which sorts mail today. Collection of items includes rural mailboxes, mail bags, carrier uniforms, multimedia theatre and an art gallery displaying works inspired by postal themes. Every Canadian stamp ever produced can be viewed on CD ROM. *Located in the Canadian Museum of Civilization. Tel. (819) 776-8200.*

Canadian Ski Museum (O)

Ski buffs can learn about Canadian ski greats such as Olympic champ Nancy Greene and cross-country pioneer Jackrabbit Johannsen. Small

museum also traces skiing from its beginnings around 3000 BC in Europe to its arrival in Canada during the last century. On display is a reproduction of a 5,000-year-old cave drawing from Norway depicting skiers and century-old ski equipment. Self-guided tours.
Mon.-Sat. 9am-5pm; Sun. 11am-5pm Admission by donation.
1960 Scott Road. Tel. (613) 722-3584.

Canadian War Museum (100/J29)

★ The country's military history comes alive through interesting and educational exhibits and more than 450,000 artifacts, from medals to tanks. A life-size diorama replicates a

The Canadian Museum of Contemporary Photography has 159,000 photos.

First World War trench. The first floor gallery looks at Canadian military history from pre-European arrival to the end of World War I; the Hall of Honour tells the personal stories of 40 military heroes; the second floor gallery explores World War II and has a large-scale model of the Normandy D-Day landing. In the Discovery Room, all ages can try on uniforms, identify artifacts or handle a colonial musket. The museum's collection of war art includes works by well-known artists such as Alex Colville and the Group of Seven. (Trivia: There hasn't been a war on Canadian soil since the War of 1812).
May-Oct.: 9:30am-5pm; Thurs. to 8pm Oct. to Apr.: 9:30am-5pm. Closed Mondays. Open Thurs. to 8

pm. Adults $4; seniors $3; students (13-17) $3; children (2-12) $2; families $9. Free admission on Sundays (9:30am-noon). Canadian veterans, military personnel and their families and members of the Canadian Forces or cadets in uniform, free. 330 Sussex Dr.; Tel. (819) 776-8600 or 1-800 555-5621.

Cumberland Heritage Village (O)

At this living history museum with more than 20 buildings, costumed interpreters and special events programming illustrate the lifestyle, occupations and industries of the lower Ottawa Valley during the early days of this century.
May-Oct.: 10am-5pm; open during Christmas season. Adults $5; seniors $3; students $3; children under 4 free. 2940 Queen St., Cumberland, 20

minutes east of Ottawa. Tel. (613) 833-3059.

Diefenbunker: Canada's Cold War Museum (0)

The chilling fear of a nuclear attack, circa 1950s, is reflected in this four-storey deep bomb shelter designed to protect the prime minister and government leaders.

May-Sept.: 10:30am-3pm daily; Sept.-mid. Nov.: weekends 12 noon-2pm. Adults $12; students & seniors $10; youth (6-15) $5. Children 5 and under free. 3911 Carp Rd., Carp (25 minutes from downtown). Tel. (613) 839-0007.

Log Farm (0)

Restored farm, dating from 1857, re-enacts life on the farm in the last century. Visitors can help with chores carried out the old fashioned way. Special events, seasonal activities, petting zoo, walking trails.

670 Cedarview Ave. East; Nepean; Tel. (613) 825-4352.

Logan Hall, Geological Survey of Canada (111/F1)

Interactive displays and videos trace the history of this organization. Its collection includes rocks, minerals, meteorites and fossils from Canada and other countries.

Mon.-Fri.: 8am-4pm. Free admission. 601 Booth St.; Tel. (613) 995-4261.

Museum of Canadian Scouting (102/P23)

Located in the lobby of the Scouts Canada building, this small museum will interest past and present Beavers, Cubs and Scouts who want to know about the history of Scouting in Canada. Photos, documents and badges from Canada and around the world.

Mon.-Fri. 9am-4:30pm. Free admission. 1345 Baseline Rd.; Tel. (613) 224-5131.

National Aviation Museum (0)

With landing gear firmly planted on the ground, more than 120 aircraft can be seen up close — from the early dreamers' machines to bombers from World War II to examples of jet engine technology. Try the Virtual Reality Hang-Glider Simulator or check out the "Full Flight" exhibit which demonstrates principles of flight.

Lost: One Astrolabe

Samuel de Champlain, the first European explorer in this region, lost a vital instrument during a portage west of Ottawa. It was called an astrolabe and it measured the altitude of planets and stars. It was recovered many years later in a farmer's field and eventually wound up in the United States. This important link to Ottawa's past was finally reclaimed by The Canadian Museum of Civilization — where you can take a look at it today.

The stunning National Gallery of Canada is a glass and granite landmark.

National and international antique aircraft include the Silver Dart, the first powered aircraft to fly in Canada in 1909. Cafe and boutique.

May-Sept.: daily 9am-5pm; Sept.-May: Tues.-Sun. 10am-5pm; Thurs. 9am-9pm; Adults $6; seniors and students $4; children 6-15, $2; children under 6 free; families $12. Aviation and Rockcliffe Parkways; Tel. (613) 993-2010 or 1-800-463-2038; www.aviation. nmstc.ca.

National Gallery of Canada (100/K29)

★ ♿ Home of the world's largest collection of Canadian art as well as excellent European and American collections. At the heart of this glass and granite landmark, designed by Moshe Safdie, is a reconstructed 19th century chapel. More than 1,200 works from the permanent collection are on view, as well as touring exhibitions from around the country and the world. Canadian artists represented include Tom Thomson and the Group of Seven, Emily Carr, Alfred Pellan, Elizabeth Wyn Wood, Jack Shadbolt and many others. Masterpieces of paintings and sculptures from the Middle Ages to present can be found in the European and American galleries; Hindu and Buddhist subjects are portrayed in the Asian galleries. A large collection of contemporary Inuit art is celebrated in stone, bone, prints, textiles and drawings. Noteworthy is the controversial Voice of Fire, an 18-foot painting by Barnett Newman, in the gallery devoted to American Expressionism. Electronic blinds and diffusing lenses protect the art from sunlight. The lower galleries are lit through an ingenious system of skylights

and mirrored shafts.
May-Oct.: daily 10am-6pm; Thurs. to 8pm year-round. Oct.-Apr.: Wed.-Sun. 10am-6pm; Admission free to permanent collection. Variable rates for special exhibitions. 380 Sussex Dr.; Tel. (613) 990-1985; national.gallery.ca.

National Library of Canada/ National Archives (100/K28)

The ultimate source of Canadian information. By law, two copies of everything published in Canada are kept here. There are more than 10 million publications. Specialized collections include Canadian theses, newspapers, official publications, rare books, literary manuscripts, children's literature and music.
Mon.-Fri. 8:30am-5pm; reading room Mon.-Fri. 8:30am-10pm; Sat. & Sun. 8am-6pm; free admission 395 Wellington Street; Tel. (613) 995-5138; www.archives.ca.

National Museum of Science and Technology (106/A5)

★ Kids and adults love this museum that mingles fun with scientific discovery. Trace the history of transportation – from old-fashioned bicycles to magnificent locomotives to modern-day space travel. Try to walk a straight line through the Crazy Kitchen or ride on the SimEx Virtual Voyage Simulator. And watching chicks hatch is fascinating.
May-Sept.: daily 9am-6pm; Fri. to 9pm. Sept.-April: Tues.-Sun., 9am-5pm, closed Mon.; Adults $6; seniors and students $5; children (6-14) $2; children under 6 free; families $12. 1867 St. Laurent Blvd. Tel. (613) 991-3044.

Nepean Museum (0)

Popular community museum has rotating exhibits, a children's discovery centre and more than 15 displays about Nepean history, dating back to the early 1790s. The Discovery Gallery is designed as a turn-of-the-century store.
Tues.-Fri. 10am-4pm; Sat. & Sun. 1-4pm. Closed Mon. Free admission. 16 Rowley Dr., Nepean; Tel. (613) 723-7936.

Great photo opportunities

Parliament Hill: Views of the Canadian Museum of Civilization and the Ottawa River waterfront

Major's Hill Park: Views of Parliament Hill and the Ottawa River waterfront

Nepean Point: Views of Parliament Hill and the Ottawa River waterfront

Canadian Museum of Civilization: Views of Parliament Hill and the waterfront, from Quebec

Victoria Island: Views of Parliament Hill, Ottawa's skyline and waterfront

Rideau Canal: Views of winding canal with skaters, bikers, Parliament Buildings and bridges

Hog's Back Falls: View of high rushing falls and water pools
     (From the Ottawa Tourism and Convention Authority)

For the active and the adventurous

The outdoors are truly great in the Capital Region

Bicycles. Snowshoes. Canoes. Runners. Skates. Mountain boots. Skis. Tent poles. The Ottawa landscape and its surroundings have been punctuated with every type of active gear. The expansive trails and outdoor activities beckon even the mildest athletes to fill their lungs with fresh air, no matter what the season. Nature bounces from the serene to the severe. You can partake in a sedentary activity, such as walking and observing nature. Or, you can really work up a sweat, with hiking, skiing or whitewater rafting.

BEACHES

Water quality is regularly checked, however some beaches close temporarily after a heavy rainfall. *For more information, call (613) 244-5678*
Britannia Bay: Ottawa River,

Thrill seekers with nerves of steel can try whitewater rafting within a 90 minute drive of downtown.

Richmond Road to Britannia Road
Meech Lake: *Gatineau Park, Parc de la Gatineau* (There are a few other beaches in this park as well).
Mooney's Bay: *Rideau River, Riverside Drive*

CAMPING

Pitch a tent and become part of the great outdoors at one of the nearby camp sites. Modern conveniences are available at some sites, while others are only for the truly adventurous. Reservations required.

The Greenbelt   (O)
Fifteen minute drive from downtown.
Tel: (613) 239-5000 or 1-800-465-1867.

La Peche Lake   (O)
For the adventurous. Canoe and kayak rentals available. 50 minute drive from Parliament Hill.
Gatineau Park. Tel.: (819) 827-2020 or 1-800-465-1867.

Le Breton Flats (99/K29)

Camping in downtown Ottawa? You bet.

Tel: (613) 236-1251 or (613) 724-6096.

Philippe Lake (0)

40 minute drive from Parliament Hill. Gatineau Park.

Tel: (819) 827-2020 or 1-800-465-1867 www.capcan.ca

Taylor Park (99/G26)

In the heart of the park. Gatineau Park, QC.

Tel: (819) 827-2020 or 1-800-465-1867 www.capcan.ca

CANOEING

Canadian Voyageur Adventures

The ultimate escape. See the Rideau and Ottawa Rivers through the eyes of the early explorers. Voyageur guides – in costume – take you on one, two or three day excursions in large stable canoes. Traditional food and equipment.

Operates year round; Tel. (613) 820-5488 or 1-800-833-5055; www.gocanoe.com

Expedition Eau Vive Laqs Inc. (100/J28)

Meet at the Museum of Civilization. Go on a guided canoe tour, or rent your own kayak or canoe. Also available: 'Tai Chi canoe' four day expedition. Group discounts available.

June-Sept.; Tel. (819) 827-4467; www.orbit.qc.ca/canoe

CAVES

Bring a flashlight and put on your waterproof shoes or boots. You're ready to go spelunking (caving). These caves are cool.... literally.

Lafleche Caves: *Val-des-Monts, QC. Tel. (819) 457-4033.*

Lusk Caves: *Gatineau Park; Tel. (819) 827-2020 or 1-800-465-1867.*

CROSS-COUNTRY SKIING

Families and beginners will love the easy trails in the Greenbelt, while Gatineau Park is geared for everyone, from beginner to expert. If you want to make it an extra long trip, Gatineau offers winter camping.

CYCLING / IN-LINE SKATING

Capital Pathway Network

Ottawa residents love their bikes. The Capital Pathway is

Gatineau Park provides a picturesque setting for camping enthusiasts.

Pedal Pushers

Over 50% of Ottawa's residents own bikes, making it a city in constant motion. With 170 kilometres of pavement, they've got one of the longest bike paths in North America. And, every weekend in the summer during Sunday Bikedays, 65 kilometres of parkways in the Capital and in Gatineau Park are closed to motorized traffic.

170 kilometres of mostly flat trails that wend their way through museums, national monuments, parks, historic sites and picnic areas.
Tel. (613) 239-5000 or 1-800-465-1867.

Sunday Bike Days

Motorized vehicles are barred from 65 kilometres of parkways in the Capital and Gatineau Park on summer Sunday mornings. But, if you're on a bike, in a wheelchair, on in-line skates, or on foot, you rule the road. Pick up a free Sunday Bikeday Map at the Capital Infocentre, opposite Parliament Hill.
Tel. (613) 239-5000 or 1-800-465-1867.

DOWNHILL SKIING

A veritable skier's paradise is within driving distance of the city. Elevation at the ski hills near Ottawa ranges from 106 to 381 metres (350 to 1,250 feet).
Ski Fortune:
Gatineau Park area (15 minutes from downtown); Tel. (819) 827-1717; www.campfortune.com
Mont Cascades:
Cantley, QC (20 minutes); Tel. (819) 827-0301; web site: www. montcascades.com

Edelweiss:
Outside Wakefield, QC (40 minutes from downtown); Tel. (819) 459-2328; www.edelweissvalley.com
Mont Ste. Marie:
Lac Ste. Marie, QC (60 minutes); Tel. (819) 467-3111 or 1-800-567-1256; www.montstemarie.com
Mont-Tremblant:
Laurentian Mountains, QC (2 hours from downtown); (3001 feet at the peak); Tel. (819) 425-8681 /1-800-567-6760; www.tremblant-.com.

FITNESS CENTRES/INDOOR POOLS

If you prefer to exercise indoors, here is a sampling:
Carleton University: *Colonel By Drive (613) 520-5631.*
University of Ottawa: *125 University Drive; Tel. (613) 562-5789.*
YMCA/YWCA: *180 Argyle Avenue; (613) 788-5000.*
Municipal Pools:
Ottawa: Tel. (613) 244-5678; 244-5300.
Hull: Tel. (819) 595-7400.

GOLF

There is a variety of golf courses for lovers of the links including:
Canadian Golf & Country Club: 27 hole course. *417 West, Exit Hwy #7 (5 mins. west of Corel Centre) Tel. (613) 780-3565.*

Pedal boating on Dows Lake makes for a relaxing summer afternoon.

Loch March:
18 hole, par 72 course. *1755 Old Carp Road, Kanata; Tel. (613) 839-5885; www.lochmarch.com*
Manderley on the Green: Championship 18 hole course, driving range. *Old Hwy 16, North Gower; Tel. (613) 489-2066 or 1-800-555-9623.*
Mont Cascades Golf:
18 hole, par 70 course in scenic setting on Gatineau River. *Chemin Mont Cascades, Cantley; Tel. (819) 459-2980; web site: www.golf.montcascades.com*
Mont Ste-Marie:
At base of ski hills with gorgeous view of Gatineau Hills.
18 holes, par 72. Tel. (819) 467-3111 or 1-800-567-1256; www. monstemarie.com

HIKING

Gatineau Park   **(98/G26)**
A scenic choice of 225 kilometres of trails allows you to make your jaunt as leisurely or as strenuous as you want. Observe the picturesque gardens and wildlife. *Tel.: (819) 827-2020.*

The Greenbelt   **(0)**
A lovely diversion. Many animals claim it as their home, including deer, moose, beavers, chipmunks and countless species of birds. Stroll along the boardwalk over the wetlands. Or, check out farms, a campground, equestrian facilities or three golf courses.
Tel. (613) 239-5000 or 1-800-465-1867.

HORSEBACK RIDING

Captiva Farms   **(0)**
Horses take you on trails that include panoramic mountains and the hills of the Gatineaus. Three or four-day tenting adventures available. Winter

activities include sleigh rides.
30 minutes from downtown. Wakefield, QC; Tel. (819) 459-2769; www3.sympatico.ca/horse-back.riding

Happy Trails Riding Stables Ltd. (0)

Get on a horse and enjoy natural wooded trails.
20 minutes from downtown; 5979 Leitrim Road, Carlsbad Springs; Tel. (613) 822-1482; www.cyberus.ca/~artmack

RENTALS

Dows Lake Pavilion (103/N27)

Summer rentals include canoes, pedalboats, kayaks, bikes and rollerblades. In winter, rent skates, sleighs, cross-country skis and snowshoes. The Pavilion has restaurants, meeting facilities and a marina.
1001 Queen Elizabeth Drive; Tel. (613) 232-1001.

Gerry & Isobel's Country Pleasures (0)

Just 20 minutes from downtown, these facilities rent bikes, snowshoes and skis. Open all year; restaurant and boutique.
14 Scott Road, Chelsea, QC; Tel. (819) 827-4341 or 1-877-827-4341.

RentABike (100/K29)

Choose from over 150, including mountain, suspension, road, tandem and kids' bikes. Infant trailers and in-line skates too. Choose an escorted tour or go on your own.
Chateau Laurier Hotel, 1 Rideau Street; Tel. (613) 241-4140; www.cyberus.ca/~renta-bike/

SKATING

The Rideau Canal (102/C6)

The world's longest skating rink (8 kilometres) has heated shelters, skate and sled rentals, and food concessions. During Winterlude, the canal hosts bed races, sleigh rides, skating and snow sculpting competitions.
Ice conditions: Tel. (613) 239-5234.

TOBOGGANING

Screaming down a snow-covered hill on a toboggan is almost a national sport. Favourite hills are: Bruce Pit Toboggan Hill, Conroy Toboggan Hill, and Green's Creek Toboggan Hill (all in the Greenbelt); and Lac des Fees Hill in Gatineau Park (where you can rent giant inner tubes).

WHITEWATER RAFTING

Want to experience the thrill of riding the rapids? These sites are at least an hour by car, but all provide accommodation (camping, etc.).
Esprit Rafting Adventures:
Davidson, QC.; Tel. (819) 683-3241 or 1-800-596-RAFT (7238); www.espritrafting.com
Ottawa Adventures Rafting:
Bryson, QC; Tel. (819) 647-3625 or 1-800-690-RAFT (7238); www. ottawaadventures.qc.ca
Owl Rafting:
Foresters Falls, Ont.; Tel. (613) 646-2263 or 1-800-461-7238 (RAFT); www.owl-mkc.ca
River Run Rafting & Paddling Centre: *Foresters Falls, Ont.; Tel. (613) 646-2501 or 1-800-267-8504; www. riverrunners.com*

Bon Appetit

International cuisine and local flavour
are on the menu daily

Ottawa is the ultimate host. As the nation's capital, it serves as the meeting place for government officials and countless convention faithful. Plus, it often assumes the duty of sole representative of Canada to its international guests. So, how can it deftly display global flavour while showcasing its own heritage? When it comes to cuisine, it's very 'well done'.

Whether grabbing a quick bite or lingering over an evening-long meal, the Ottawa region has a tasty selection of restaurants on its menu: bistros, cafes, intimate settings, cultural cuisine and noisy diners are scattered throughout busy city streets and remote hideaways. You can also eat at most bars, some of which provide entertainment as well.

The French Canadian in-

During summer, Ottawa's numerous outdoor cafes do a bustling business.

fluence is reflected in the food. Rich sauces, delicate crepes and exceptional service can be found in many of the region's fine French restaurants. The ratio of these elegant establishments — some of which feature vegetables plucked from nearby gardens or mushrooms gathered from the Gatineau Park — is higher than in most cities due to the volume of elite business travellers.

This region is also proud to offer a veritable cornucopia of international fare: French, Japanese, Italian, Mexican, Chinese, Thai, Indian and much more. Not feeling adventurous? That's okay. There are plenty of eateries that serve up delicious Canadian and American fare; and, of course, there's always fast food. Whatever your taste or craving, there's a restaurant waiting to serve you.

Good service merits a 15 per cent tip. Exceptional 20 per cent. Taxes on the meal bump

MARCO POLO SELECTION: RESTAURANTS

1 L'Oree du Bois
Secluded wooded setting
and fine French cuisine
(page 48)

2 Big Daddy's Crab Shack
A taste of New Orleans
and sounds of Dixieland
jazz (page 48)

3 Chez Jean Pierre
Intimate, elegant and
impeccably prepared
food (page 46)

4 Feleena's
Olé! For those who love
a taste of Mexico
(page 50)

5 The Mill
Great steakhouse and
prime rib in a historic
setting (page 51)

6 Mamma Teresa's
Mamma knows best
about great Italian food
(page 51)

7 Blue Cactus Bar & Grill
Casual, trendy dining with
a Tex-Mex flavour
(page 48)

8 Courtyard Restaurant
Intimate setting and fine
food in a historic stone
building (page 46)

9 Zak's Diner
Burgers, shakes and fries
in a '50s style setting
(page 53)

10 Savana Cafe
Tasty Thai and Caribbean
specialties (page 51)

up the price, so it is acceptable to tip on the subtotal.

CATEGORY 1

From $30 per person for a three course meal. Reservations are recommended.

Café Henry Burger (100/J29)
Since 1922, Cafe Henry Burger has maintained its first-rate reputation for exquisite seasonal French cuisine. Their extensive wine list will impress. During warm weather, enjoy their outdoor terrace with its open pit barbecue. Across from the Museum of Civilization.

69 Laurier Ave.; Tel. (819) 777-5646.

Chez Jean Pierre (104/L29)
★ Spoil yourself at this refined French restaurant. The food, including rack of lamb, seafood, and mushrooms from the Gatineau (in season) is magnifique. The service is excellent. Look closely for the restaurant's street sign. The entrance is so unassuming, it's easy to miss.
210 Somerset W, Tel. (613) 235-9711.

Courtyard Restaurant (100/K29)
★ Intimate fine dining upstairs in historic stone building.

House specialties include rack of lamb, Beef Tenderloin Wellington and Atlantic salmon and mouth-watering desserts such as chocolate and bourbon tart. Attentive service. More casual dining on outdoor patio.

21 George St. (Byward Market), Tel. (613) 241-1516.

Hull-Chelsea-Wakefield Sunset Dinner Train   (0)

Moving scenery and French cuisine make this a truly unique dining experience. The train, which leaves Hull station every Friday and Saturday evening from June to September, takes you through the beautiful Gatineau hills.

165 Devault St., Hull   For reservations, call (819) 778-7246.

Hy's Steakhouse   (100/K29)

Not just great steak, Hy's offers lobster, rack of lamb and other scrumptious dishes. The atmosphere, with its dark panelling and white linen, is comfortable and elegant all at once.

170 Queen St.; Tel. (613) 234-4545.

Japanese Village   (100/K29)

Food also serves as entertainment here as exuberant chefs prepare sushi, teppanyaki and other dishes at your table. Great service.

170 Laurier Ave. W. Tel. (613) 236-9519.

Le Baccara   (100/G28)

Located in the Casino de Hull, Le Baccara is already earning a reputation as one of Quebec's finest restaurants.

Casino de Hull, Tel. (819) 772-6210.

Le Café, National Arts Centre   (100/K29)

★ ♫ Dinner and live entertainment can be enjoyed under the same roof at The National Arts Centre. Le Café is a classy setting with a selective offering of unique Canadian dishes. Excellent service. The view of the Rideau Canal adds to the atmosphere. *53 Elgin, Tel. (613) 594-5127.*

Le Jardin   (100/K29)

The ambience of the 19th century Victorian home that is Le Jardin is a perfect match for the fine French cuisine that is served here.

Open for dinner seven days a week. 127 York St.; Tel. (613) 241-1424.

Les Muses   (100/J29)

♫ Dining at the museum is elegant and unique. And the Sunday brunch package is amazing! It includes a fabulous selection of entrees, smoked fish, salads and desserts, plus Imax-Omnimax theatre tickets, and a helicopter tour of the city.

Canadian Museum of Civilization, 100 Laurier, Hull Tel. (819) 776-7009.

Le Tartuffe   (0)

Fine French dining is made even more special with Le Tartuffe's grand selection of seasonal appetizers and entrees, using only local

produce. Guaranteed to impress.
133 Notre Dame, Hull; Tel. (819) 776-6424.

L'Orée du Bois (0)

★ Tucked away in the Gatineau Park, this quietly elegant restaurant offers fine French and regional cuisine in a pastoral setting. Fresh herbs are available from their gardens (outdoor and indoor) all year long. Appetizers and entrees are set on the plate in such artistic style, they look camera-ready.
15 Kingsmere Rd., Old Chelsea, Quebec; Tel. (819) 827-0332.

The Marble Works Restaurant (100/K29)

Restored 1866 heritage building offers intimate but casual dining and a modern renovated open kitchen. Excellent steak and prime rib. Sunday brunch. Murder mystery Saturday nights. Open daily except Saturday lunch.
14 Waller Street; (613) 241-6764.

CATEGORY 2

From $15 to $30 per person for dinner.

Al's Steakhouse and Seafood (100/L29)

Highly recommended by many Ottawa residents. Generous portions of meat, potatoes and seafood have made this a favourite for over 25 years. Pricier meals too.
Two locations: 327 Elgin (613) 233-7111; 3817 Richmond Rd.; Tel. (613) 828-8349.

Banco (100/J29)

After playing the tables at the casino, check out the winning buffet table or the varied menu. *Casino de Hull (819) 772-6220.*

Big Daddy's Crab Shack (104/L29)

★ Fun and funky New Orleans-style restaurant with Dixieland jazz on the sound system and mouth-watering mussels, crab, lobster and more on the menu. Famous for its oyster bar. The jalapeno pasta and filet mignon are delicious too. Hint: try the creole-style house salad dressing.
Two locations: 780 Baseline (at Fisher) (613) 228-7011; 339 Elgin (at Waverly); Tel. (613) 569-JAZZ.

The Black Tomato (100/K29)

With CD players and disks available to patrons, the atmosphere here wavers from soothing to hip to earthy. It's a casual place with a varied menu that offers wine recommendations for each entree. Read a music magazine, available at the front, while you eat.
11 George (corner of Sussex); Tel. (613) 789-8123.

Blue Cactus Bar & Grill (100/K29)

★ ❀ Mexican, Cajun and Tex-Mex dishes in Texas-size portions include Voodoo chicken, Sante Fe pizza, steak, fajitas and more. Colourful southern decor; famous for the nachos and tasty margaritas.
2 Byward Market, Tel. (613) 241-7061.

Bravo Bravo (100/K29)

Cluttered, clean and inviting, the bright Tuscan decor is a perfect setting for pasta, pizza, risotto and antipasto. Bar, pool tables, martini & cigar lounge, and an inviting outdoor terrace complete the buoyant mood.
292 Elgin Street; Tel. (613) 233-7525.

Café Baci (100/K29)

European-style cafe specializes in tasty Italian dishes.
297 Dalhousie (ByWard Market); Tel. (613) 241-2224.

Casablanca Resto (100/K29)

This restaurant re-creates the aura of the Humphrey Bogart cinematic classic of the same name while serving fine Moroccan and North American cuisine.
41 Clarence (ByWard Market); Tel. (613) 789-7855.

Caveau de Szechwan (100/K29)

Chic Art Deco restaurant has 'all-you-can-eat' dinners featuring authentic Hunan and Szechuan cuisine.
129 York St. (ByWard Market); Tel. (613) 562-2882.

Clair de Lune (100/K29)

A favourite among food critics, this well-established French eatery is also popular with media and political types.
81-B Clarence (ByWard Market); Tel. (613) 241-2200.

Coasters Seafood (100/K29)

Sit down to a plate of mussels... or pizza...or try Coasters' salmon burger or fish steak. Nice selection of wines, beers and spirits.
54 York (ByWard Market); Tel. (613) 241-4954.

The Creperie (100/K29)

A French classic, the crepe can be stuffed with entree items (such as chicken, beef, veggies and seafood) or dessert items. Hungarian Chocolate Nut Crepe, Strawberries Romanoff Crepe and Banana Split Crepe are a few choices.
47 York, ByWard Market; Tel. (613) 241-8805.

D'Arcy McGee's (100/K29)

Molly Malone's Mussels, Fionn MacCool's Wings, and Mrs. Brady's Bread Pudding are three of the choices at this authentic Irish pub. Whiskey, port, and of course, Guinness.
44 Sparks St.; Tel. (613) 230-4433.

In the Marco Polo Spirit

Marco Polo was the first true world traveller. He travelled with peaceful intentions, forging links between the East and the West. His aim was to discover the world and to explore different cultures and environments without changing or disrupting them. He is an excellent role model for the 21st-century traveller. Wherever we travel we should show respect for other peoples and the natural world.

The Blue Cactus in the ByWard Market serves up Tex-Mex cuisine.

Eggspectation (104/L29)

Egg-sellent and eleggant eatery isn't limited to crepes and eggs Benedict. Get waffles, pasta, fish, salads and burgers too.

171 Bank St. (corner Laurier Ave.); Tel. (613) 569-6505.

The Empire Grill (100/K29)

♣ A sophisticated New York-style bistro that's part restaurant, part martini bar and part night club. It all adds up to a hip, happening place that serves great food.

47 Clarence St. (Byward Market); Tel. (613) 241-1343.

Feleena's (104/N29)

Spicy. Crunchy. Cool. One of the best places to nosh on authentic Mexican cuisine.

742 Bank St. (The Glebe); Tel. (613) 233-2010.

The Fish Market (100/K29)

Specializing in fine fish dishes for 20 years. Casual Maritime decor. Live lobster and fresh trout tanks.

54 York St. (Byward Market); Tel. (613) 241-3474.

Flippers (108/A2)

If you're a seafood fanatic, you'll love the fresh oysters, smoked salmon, live lobster, calamari and more. Pasta and other dishes too.

823 Bank St. (The Glebe); Tel. (613) 232-2703.

Les Fougeres (0)

〰 Unparalleled atmosphere inside and out. Nestled in the Chelsea region of Meech Lake, it offers traditional French Canadian cuisine in a wood-land setting 15-minutes from downtown.

783 Route 105, Chelsea, QC (819) 827-8942.

Mamma Grazzi's   (100/K29)

A taste of Old World Italian cuisine in a historic courtyard. The fresh pasta and thin-crust pizzas are magnifico.

25 George (Byward Market); Tel. (613) 241-8656.

Mamma Teresa Ristorante   (104/L29)

★ Thirty years ago, Giuliano Boselli and his mother, Mamma Teresa, brought a little bit of northern Italy to Ottawa. Italian cuisine and friendly service are still a treasured part of this region.

300 Somerset Street W. (corner of O'Connor); Tel. (613) 236-3023.

Maxwell's Bistro   (104/L29)

Comfortable and classy with an international menu that features gourmet pizza, an oyster bar, vegetarian specials and homemade desserts. After dinner, visit the night club upstairs.

340 Elgin; Tel. (613) 232-5771.

The Mill   (100/K28)

★ Housed in a magnificent stone building renovated for Canada's centennial year, The Mill serves mouth-watering prime rib. Chicken, pasta and seafood dishes too.

555 Ottawa River Parkway; Tel. (613) 237-1311.

Nagina Indian Cuisine   (100/K30)

For over two decades, Ottawa has enjoyed the exotic tastes of Tandoori cuisine. The Indian buffet is the largest in town.

217 Rideau St.; Tel. (613) 562-0060.

Royal Thai   (100/K30)

Thai chefs serve up exceptional MSG-free food from a varied menu.

272 Dalhousie; Tel. (613) 562-8818.

Sante Restaurant   (100/K29)

A taste of something different. This restaurant and gallery creates innovative dishes with Thai, Caribbean and Mediterranean flavours.

45 Rideau St. (at Sussex); Tel. (613) 241-7113.

Savana Cafe   (104/L28)

★ Bright and casual decor in this restored house. East meets west in delicious Thai and Caribbean items.

431 Gilmour St.; Tel. (613) 233-9159.

Silk Roads   (100/K29)

Authentic Afghan cuisine includes vegetarian dishes as well as kabobs of lamb, chicken, beef and quail. *47 William St. (ByWard Market); Tel. (613) 241-4254.*

Suisha Gardens   (104/L29)

An original, yet traditional, place to enjoy Japanese cuisine. Watch little boats float by in the sushi bar, each one displaying tempting delicacies. Private tatami rooms available.

208 Slater St. (off Bank); Tel. (613) 236-9602.

Thai Garden Restaurant (100/K29)

Features authentic Thai cuisine.

246 Queen St.; Tel. (613) 234-7161.

Customers line up to order one of Beaver Tails' tasty pastries.

VietNam Palace (104/L28)

Warm, friendly service and exotic cuisine without MSG. Create your own meat, veggie and seafood spring rolls right at your table.
819 Somerset W.; Tel. (613) 238-6758.

Vineyards Wine Bar & Bistro (100/K29)

Sure, this award-winning wine bar in a candlelit cellar is the perfect spot to raise a glass of vino, imported beer or malt whiskey, but you can also order sirloin steak, salad, and other things to go with your drinks. *54 York St. (Byward Market); Tel. (613) 241-4270.*

Vittoria Trattoria (100/K29)

Casual trattoria specializes in gourmet pizzas heated in wood-burning oven. Award-winning wine list.
35 William (ByWard Market); Tel. (613) 789-8959.

CATEGORY 3

Under $15 per person

Buffalo Charlie's (100/K29)

Finger food like burgers, ribs, fajitas and more; plus steak, pizza, and pasta. Sunday buffet. *Three locations: 33 Clarence (613) 241-4811; 2525 Carling Ave. (613) 828-8988; 2269 Riverside Drive (613) 247-1122.*

Café Wim & Gallery (100/K29)

Local artists' work adorns the walls in this charming Dutch café that emphasizes, but is not limited to, vegetarian dishes. *537 Sussex Drive; Tel. (613) 241-1771.*

James St. Feed Co.   (104/L29)
❀ Rumour has it the best chicken wings in town can be found here. Popular with students.
390 Bank St.; Tel. (613) 563-4700.

Mexicali Rosa's   (104/M29)
Mexican fare that's so popular, there are four locations.
The Globe: 895 Bank (613) 236-9499, Downtown: 200 Rideau (613) 241-7044, West end: 975 Richmond Rd. (613) 722-4692, Dow's Lake: 1001 Queen E. Dr. (613) 234-8156.

Oregano's   (100/K29)
Oh joy! Oregano's is well known for its pasta, pizza and salad. Fabulous desserts too. Great place to people-watch in the summer.
74 George St. (Byward Market); (613) 241-5100.

Pancho Villa   (100/M29)
Mexican and Tex-Mex dishes include fresh guacamole, fajitas, hot tamales and more. Sunday brunch.
8 - 361 Elgin (at Frank); Tel. (613) 234-8872.

Zak's Diner   (100/K29)
★ Food is fun in this 1950s style diner. Enjoy burgers, sandwiches, and shakes amidst pink, turquoise and chrome decor. 1950s memorabilia with tabletop jukeboxes too.
16 Byward Market; Tel. (613) 241-2401.

FOR THE SWEET TOOTH

Beaver Tails   (100/K29)
It's not fancy, but this place is extremely popular with locals and tourists. Yummy warm pastries topped with scrumptious ingredients. Flavours include Chocolate Hazelnut, Classic Cinnamon & Sugar, and Garlic Butter & Cheese. Mmmmmm.
ByWard Market; and along the Rideau Canal during Winterlude.

Piccolo Grande   (100/K29)
What's your favourite flavour of ice cream? You'll find it here, as well as soup, salad, sandwiches, pasta and cappuccino.
55 Murray St. (Byward Market); Tel. (613) 241-2909.

A Sweet Tale of Success

Every Ottawa resident — and scores of tourists — know about Beaver Tails. People will stand in line in the summer heat or the bitter cold just to experience the tasty pastry topped with sinful sweets or savoury ingredients. It started in 1978 when the Hooker family opened the first Beaver Tails in the ByWard Market. It was so popular, they've built over 50 more across North America. And now, with Central America and Asia about to experience the taste sensation, the company is still as busy as a...well, you know.

Endless choice

*From open air markets to climate-controlled malls,
Ottawa has a vast array of shopping haunts.*

In this city, you don't just run out and buy something, you choose your setting. There are the clean lines, familiar giants and small shops in any of the abundant malls; then there's the bustle of the open air ByWard market, a great place to soak up village atmosphere in the heart of the city; of course, there are the cultural pockets such as Chinatown and Little Italy; and Canada's first pedestrian mall is plunked right downtown. The choices don't end here. You're sure to find many more sidewalk boutiques, out-of-the-way places and neighbourhood clusters that have exactly what you're looking for – and what you've never seen before.

Hours of operation vary, however many stores are open until 9pm Monday to Friday, until 6pm on Saturdays and from 12-5pm on Sundays.

From major malls to specialty shops, from expensive to bargain-priced, Ottawa is sure to please.

Don't forget that a 15 per cent tax is added to the ticket price – excluding books and most groceries – but Americans should make up for it with the favourable exchange rate. The best time to scout for bargains is at the end of a season when stores try to clear out their stock. And on Boxing Day. You can check out Ottawa's variety of shopping areas and centres on the web site, www.ottawakiosk.com.

DISTRICTS

ByWard Market   (100/K29)

Where do you go when you want a chic hat, a zucchini and unique artwork? With its roots in the 19th century, this bustling marketplace likes to mix it up, offering fresh vegetables, maple syrup, fish, and flowers alongside artwork, jewellery, housewares and clothing. Prices range from bargain basement to très elegante. Some merchants keep their doors open late in the

MARCO POLO SELECTION: SHOPPING

1 The Bay
A Canadian institution for 300 years (page 57)

2 Canada's Four Corners
Large selection of Native arts and crafts at this bustling souvenir shop (page 57)

3 Christmas Shoppe on William
Festive season delights all year round (page 59)

4 Nicholas Hoare
For lovers of of the written word (page 57)

5 McIntosh & Watts
Fine china, crystal and much more (page 60)

6 Sassy Bead Co.
Create your own unique jewellery (page 63)

7 Giraffe African Arts
Traditional and contemporary African arts, crafts and instruments (page 60)

8 La Cache
Difficult to define, easy to enjoy (page 57)

9 Cows
Bovine-inspired gift items and great ice cream (page 59)

10 Richard Robinson
The place for fashion trend setters (page 59)

evening if the weather is pleasant and the pedestrian traffic is busy.
Just east of Parliament Hill off Sussex Drive.

The Glebe (104/N29)
The village atmosphere of The Glebe teeters from funky to upscale, and in some cases it combines both in its eclectic mix of specialty shops, services and restaurants.
Along Bank Street from the Queensway to the Rideau Canal.

Somerset Heights (103/L27)
The city's only Asian marketplace offers more than Chinese herbs and great Asian cuisine. It's got everything from the exotic to the everyday. Good variety of stores and services nestled amidst a heritage landscape.
Between Booth and Preston Streets on Somerset.

Sparks Street Pedestrian Mall (100/K29)
This outdoor mall is closed to traffic and has more than 45 stores, services and restaurants. It's Canada's first pedestrian mall.
One block south of Parliament Hill at Bank and Queen St.

ANTIQUES

The Antique Shoppe (104/N29)
18th and 19th century furniture from Canada, the U.S., and Europe.
750 Bank Street (The Glebe).

Donohue & Bousquet (104/M29)
Large collection of antique silver and Old Sheffield Plate.
27 Hawthorne Ave. (between Pretoria Bridge and Main Street).

Ottawa Antique Market (104/M29)
Antique buffs will love exploring this treasure trove just 10 minutes from Parliament Hill.
1179A Bank Street.

A BIT OF EVERYTHING

La Cache (104/N29)
A variety of earthy, upscale goods for your home, table and clothes closet. Blankets, kids' clothes, pottery. A lot of choice in limited space.
763 Bank Street (The Glebe).

Masala (100/K29)
Handcrafted sterling silver, semi-precious stones, gorgeous clothing, carvings and curios.
17-B York Street (ByWard Market).

BOOKSHOPS

Nicholas Hoare (100/K29)
The love of the page is clearly evident in the surroundings, stock, and knowledgeable staff at this popular book store.
419 Sussex Dr. (ByWard Market).

Place Bell Books (100/K29)
This book lovers' haven specializes in city and country travel books and maps; plus a variety of general interest books.
175 Metcalfe Street.

CANADIANA

Canada's Four Corners (100/K29)
★ The largest handicrafts and souvenir store in Canada stocks a wide range of Native-inspired crafts and clothing.
93 Sparks St. (Sparks Street Mall at Metcalfe).

Canadian Geographic Boutique (100/K29)
This shop compresses all things Canadian within its walls, making souvenir shopping a cinch.
Two locations: 39 McArthur Ave. (off the Vanier Parkway); the Rideau Centre.

Canal Company (100/K29)
History and humour are in abundance in this 19th-century-style general store.
89 Murray St. (ByWard Market).

The Inuit Artists' Shop (100/K29)
Beautiful carvings, dolls, prints and other art inspired by nature and tradition are featured in this shop and gallery. Elements of nature often comprise the art; some pieces are made of stone, antler, bone, etc.
16 Clarence St. (ByWard Market).

The Snow Goose Ltd. (100/K29)
Dreamcatchers, Inuit prints and carvings, Native jewellery and leather goods made by artists from across Canada.
83 Sparks St. (Sparks Street Mall).

DEPARTMENT STORES

The Bay (100/K29)
★ For a place that's been

around for over 300 years, The Bay is still a thoroughly modern place to shop. Designer names abound, as do practical and exquisite items. The grandaddy of department stores is also the exclusive distributor of Wayne Gretzky fashions.

Four locations: The Rideau Centre, Bayshore Shopping Centre, Place D'Orleans Shopping Centre, St. Laurent Centre.

FASHION

Brio (104/N29)
Buying a bathing suit is a pleasure in this shop.
877 Bank (The Glebe).

Holt Renfrew (100/K29)
The name Holt Renfrew has become synonymous with high class fashion. Over 100 of the world's most renowned designer labels — including Holt Renfrew's own.
240 Sparks Street.

O'Shea's Market Ireland (100/K29)
All things Irish can be found in this exclusive Ottawa shop. Gorgeous sweaters, unique gifts and jewellery.
91 Sparks St. (Sparks Street Mall).

Penelope's (104/N29)
Merchandise in this store is Canadian-made; some made in Ontario; some designed by the owner. Coats, sweaters, jewellery and accessories.
815 Bank St. (The Glebe).

Puerto Del Sol Swimwear (100/K29)
Dozens of swimwear lines from around the world are

The downtown Sparks Street Mall was Canada's first pedestrian mall.

featured here. Broad range of sizes and expert advice; goggles and beach shoes too.
335 Cumberland Street (ByWard Market).

Richard Robinson (100/K29)
Marlen Cowpland, the flashy Ottawa celebrity and wife of Corel Corp. magnate Michael Cowpland, is as famous for her fashions as her presence. This is where she buys some of her most notorious outfits.
447 Sussex Drive (ByWard Market).

Sheperd's (100/K29)
Unique clothing, accessories and jewellery. Upscale look at reasonable prices.
Rideau Centre, Bayshore Shopping Centre.

FLEA MARKETS

Stittsville Market (0)
This huge indoor-outdoor market is overflowing with great finds.
6176 Hazeldean Rd. (10 mins. west of Ottawa, Exit 140, left on Terry Fox Dr., right at Hazeldean Rd.) Sundays only 9am-5pm.

FURS

The fur trade still goes on today, in a sense.

Burkholder Furs (104/L29)
This furrier, established in 1910 and centrally located, has a generous selection of Canadian fur fashions.
119 Bank St. (near Slater).

Dworkin Furs (101/K30)
Up to 1,000 furs — from Canada and around the world — are stocked in this boutique that opened in 1901.
256 Rideau St.

Pat Flesher Furs (101/L29)
Established in 1929, this shop specializes in the three-pound fur coat. Mink, beaver, fox, raccoon, sable and more.
437 Cooper St. (Between Bank and Kent).

GIFTS

Christmas & Candles (100/K29)
Deck the halls with floating candles and celebrate the festive season year-round with goods from this shop. Two lovely ideas in one place.
481 Sussex Dr. (2 blocks south of National Gallery).

Christmas in the Capital (104/L29)
Delight in the spirit of Christmas year-round with keepsakes, gifts and ornaments.
231 Elgin St.

The Christmas Shoppe on William (100/K29)
No matter what the season, the magic and charm of the North Pole are contained here.
71 William St. (ByWard Market).

Cows (100/K29)
Spot your favourite bovine-inspired souvenir, from hats to mugs to t-shirts, in this udderly fun gift shop which also is famous for its ice cream.
43 Clarence St. (ByWard Market).

The ByWard Market has a farmers' market and many specialty shops.

East Wind (104/N29)
Crafts from China, Japan and Korea.
794 Bank St. (The Glebe).

Giraffe African Arts (100/K29)
Traditional and contemporary African art, crafts, jewellery and musical instruments.
19 Clarence St. at Sussex (ByWard Market).

Mastermark Pewter (100/K29)
Solidly elegant picture frames, tankards, figurines, candlesticks, dishes and more.
Three locations: Rideau Centre, Carlingwood Mall, St. Laurent Shopping Centre.

McIntosh & Watts (102/B5)
This Ottawa institution has spread to include five locations, backing up its 90-year success of selling fine china, silverware, crystal, flatware, collectibles and Christmas decorations.

Five locations: 193 Sparks St., St. Laurent Shopping Centre, Place d'Orleans Shopping Centre, Bayshore Shopping Centre, 2417 Holly Lane (warehouse store).

National Gallery of Canada Gift Shop (100/K29)
Excellent prints, art books, artistic souvenirs. Oh yeah, the Gallery's spectacular too.
380 Sussex Drive.

Oh Yes Ottawa (100/K29)
Oh Canada! Unique clothing and gifts.
50 Rideau St., Rideau Centre.

HOUSEHOLD

C.A. Paradis (104/N29)
This is a supplier of professional-quality kitchen goods for the restaurant industry, but wanna-be chefs are welcome too. Knives, fine crystal and

cookware.
1314 Bank Street.

Domus (100/K29)
Shop for your kitchen, then enjoy something from the adjoining bistro.
85 Murray (ByWard Market).

The Glebe Emporium (104/N29)
Upscale kitchen gadgets and accessories. Paderno cookware on the top floor.
724 Bank St. (The Glebe).

Ma Cuisine (100/K29)
Gadgets, gizmos, cookware and glassware for every cook.
269 Dalhousie St. (ByWard Market).

Zone (100/K29)
Candles, lamps and a large range of contemporary accessories for the home.
471 Sussex Dr. (ByWard Market).

JEWELLERY

Alyea's Jewellers Ltd. (100/K29)
Custom-designed jewellery as well as repairs and restoration. Estate jewellery and gems too.
50 Sparks Street.

Jublilee Fine Jewellers (100/K29)
Exclusive designer collections of 18 karat gold and platinum jewellery, diamonds and pearls.
3rd floor, Rideau Centre.

KIDS

Glebe Side Kids (104/N29)
You'll gasp at the fine designs for the younger generation–

and at the prices.
793 Bank St. (The Glebe).

Kids Cosy Cottons (100/K29)
Outfit your kids in cool cottons or warm knits.
517 Sussex Drive (ByWard Market).

Mrs. Tiggy Winkle's (104/N29)
Toys, games and puzzles will delight in this bright, colourful store.
Four locations: 809 Bank (The Glebe), Rideau Centre, Place D'Orleans, Bayshore Shopping Centre.

MALLS

Bayshore Shopping Centre (0)
The Bay is here, as well as over 160 other stores.
At the intersection of Richmond Road and the Queensway.

L'esplanade Laurier Shopping Mall (0)
Indoor shopping that has something for everyone.
171 Bank Street.

Place D'Orleans Shopping Centre (0)
Over 200 stores (including WalMart and the Bay) in this mall located just east of downtown. Parking is free and access is easy.
Eastbound, just off the Queensway.

The Rideau Centre (100/K29)
A variety of stores, restaurants, clubs, galleries, theatres, attractions, hotels and services. Included is the familiar (The Bay, Chapters) and the unique.

The Glebe offers an eclectic mix of shops, services and restaurants.

Beside the Rideau Canal and National Arts Centre.

St. Laurent Centre (O)

For up-to-the-minute fashion, toys and activities, this is the place. This shopping centre houses familiar names like Sears, The Bay, Toys R Us, Club Monaco, Athletes World and The Gap. It also has movie theatres and a virtual reality complex. *Downtown off the*

Queensway at St. Laurent Boulevard.

World Exchange Plaza (100/K29)

You'll find over 60 stores and services in this downtown plaza. Plus movie theatres, restaurants, conference facilities, underground parking, an outdoor amphitheatre and an amazing food court.

Albert and Metcalfe Streets.

SPECIALTY STORES

Annabelle's
The Angel Store   (100/K29)
Heavenly collection of angels, incense, candles and crystals. On-site massage, aromatherapy and spiritual counselling.
1200F Wellington St.

Bank Street Framing   (104/N29)
Frames as unique and artsy as the work inside it.
728 Bank St.

Belle de Provence   (100/K29)
Bath and beauty boutique inspired by the south of France carries natural soap, perfume and cosmetics, plus pottery and food from Provence. Fabric and antique furniture too.
80 George Street; (613) 789-2552.

Comerford's Cigar
Store   (104/N29)
Since 1948, long before smoking stogies became trendy. Giftware and periodicals too.
124 Bank St. (The Glebe).

Lush Handmade
Cosmetics   (100/K29)
A cosmetics store done deli-style. Pick facial cleansers, toiletries, bath products from bins.
43 William St. (ByWard Market).

The Papery   (104/N29)
Write. Wrap. Fold. Create. You won't want to crumple this stuff.
850 Bank St. (The Glebe).

The Sassy Bead
Company   (104/N29)
Create your own unique jewellery from thousands of colourful beads, stones and accessories.
Two locations: 757 Bank St. (The Glebe); 11 William St. (ByWard Market).

The Tea Party   (100/K29)
Wrap your hands around a steaming mug of coffee at home or in the store. Hundreds of teas and coffees, as well as the paraphernalia to go with them.
119 York Street (ByWard Market).

Of Mouse and Men
It was the ultimate clash of American and Canadian icons. On the north side: the Mounties. On the south: Disney. Patriotic Canadians were shocked in 1994 when Disney – the corporate giant that created Mickey Mouse – was chosen to handle marketing of the Mounties' image. But, after five years, the partnership ended. The Mounted Police Foundation claims Disney was the experienced marketing teacher it needed at the time. Figures indicate that revenues and royalties didn't meet expectations. In any case, the Mounties were ready to let go of Mickey's three-fingered hand and try it on their own.

Capital accommodation

No matter where you stay, you're close to history and to modern-day conveniences.

Whether you choose a cozy bed & breakfast, a stately time-honoured hotel, or a familiar chain, you're not far from the power of Parliament Hill, the magnificence of nature, or the lure of the mall.

If you're not sure exactly where to stay, call the Capital Infocentre at 1-800-465-1867 and ask for Accommodation. Most hotels are represented here so the centre can book your reservation, as well as recommend package deals which could include restaurants, museums and tours. If you've left things to the last minute, you can drop into the Capital Infocentre in person, across from Parliament Hill. It will have complete listings of which hotels can make immediate accommodations, often offering a money-saving

The stately Chateau Laurier is Ottawa's very own French Renaissance-style castle.

deal due to the time crunch.

Ottawa plays host to a multitude of conventions, especially from mid-May until the end of June, and again in mid-September. It's always more of a challenge, albeit never impossible, to get accommodation during these busy periods. Even July and August – very busy months for tourism – aren't as clogged with out-of-towners as the convention months.

You might see the Ontario SuperHost symbol in some hotels. This is a province-wide customer service program that the hotel staff would have taken, making the level of service consistent and usually better than standard.

Families may prefer to look for hotels with suites, which usually offer separate bedrooms. This no doubt capitalizes on the privacy – as well as the sanity – factor.

Please note that at most downtown hotels, you have to pay for parking.

MARCO POLO SELECTION: HOTELS

1 Chateau Laurier
History, elegance and luxury in a prime location (page 69)

2 Westin Hotel
Contemporary comforts with spectacular views (page 68)

3 Lord Elgin Hotel
Modern amenities in historic central setting (page 69)

4 Brighton House B&B
Elegant Edwardian houses in the Glebe (page 68)

5 Radisson Hotel
Newly renovated with stunning views (page 67)

6 Le Chateau Cartier
Golf resort with European country charm (page 67)

7 Gausthaus Switzerland Inn
Small inn atmosphere with big hotel efficiency (page 68)

8 Les Suites
Downtown location, spacious suites (page 67)

9 Minto Place Suite Hotel
Catering to executives and family vacationers (page 67)

10 Sheraton Ottawa
Modern 236 room hotel catering to families (page 68)

GROUP A HOTELS

From $100 per night and up

Albert at Bay Suite Hotel (104/L28)

Modern suite hotel in heart of the city. One and two bedroom suites, full kitchens. Accredited child and youth friendly; good for business travellers too.
196 rooms; 435 Albert St. (corner of Albert and Bay); Tel. (613) 238-8858 or 1-800-267-6644.

The Aristocrat Hotel & Suites (104/L29)

Newly renovated facility close to ByWard Market, Parliament Hill, National Arts Centre, etc. Popular with government types.
100 rooms; 131 Cooper St.; Tel. (613) 236-7500 or 1-800-563-5634.

Best Western Victoria Park Suites (104/L28)

Classy hotel with penthouse, fitness centre and semi- and one bedroom suites with kitchenettes. Meeting facilities for up to 120 people.
100 rooms; 377 O'Connor St.; Tel. (613) 567-7275 or 1-800-465-7275.

Cartier Place & Towers Suite Hotels (104/L29)

Large hotel with all the amenities, including fitness centre, pool, gift shop, children's services, etc.
254 rooms; 180 Cooper St.; Tel. (613) 236-5000 or 1-800-236-8399.

Courtyard Marriot (100/K29)

Renovated low-rise hotel with

oversized rooms, king and queen beds, fitness centre and indoor/outdoor pool in heart of ByWard Market. Family friendly. Minutes walk to major attractions.

183 rooms. 350 Dalhousie St.; Tel. (613) 241-1000 or 1-800-341-2210.

Crowne Plaza (104/L28)
Newly renovated, with the city's largest hotel fitness centre, complete with indoor pool. Steps from Parliament Buildings.
411 rooms; 101 Lyon St.; Tel. (613) 237-3600 or 1-800-567-3600.

Delta Ottawa Hotel & Suites (100/K28)
Modern downtown hotel that's great for families. One and two bedroom suites with kitchenettes and balconies. Two-storey indoor water slide and Leisure Land, Children's Creative Centre, in-room movies and Nintendo.
328 rooms; 361 Queen St.; Tel. (613) 238-6000 or 1-800-268-1133.

Le Chateau Cartier Hotel & Golf Resort (0)
★ ⚜ Combine business with pleasure at this grand resort. The picturesque 18-hole golf course is the focal point, but there are many other activities: tennis, squash, racquetball, basketball, aerobics centre, bike rentals, heated pool, whirlpool, sauna and steam rooms. 15 minutes from downtown.
129 rooms; 1170 chemin Aylmer, Aylmer, QC; Tel.: (819) 777-1088/ 1-800-807-1088.

Les Suites (101/K30)
★ Downtown suites with spacious one and two bedroom units, indoor pool and fitness centre, in-room movies and Nintendo games.
243 rooms; 130 Besserer St.; Tel. (613) 232-2000 or 1-800-267-1989.

Minto Place Suites (100/L29)
★ The city's first suites hotel still provides great service for business executives or for vacationing families. Services, restaurants and banking on lower level concourse.
417 rooms; 433 Laurier Ave. W.; Tel. (613) 232-2020 or 1-800-267-3377.

Novotel Ottawa (100/K29)
Modern rooms in central location with pool and fitness centre.
281 rooms; 33 Nicholas St.; Tel. (613) 230-3033 or 1-800-NOV-OTEL.

Radisson Ottawa Centre (100/K29)
★ ⚜ Recently renovated top to bottom, with spacious, tastefully decorated rooms and convenient location. City's only revolving restaurant (La Ronde) provides spectacular views of the Parliament Buildings, Ottawa River, etc. Well-equipped fitness centre.
478 rooms; 100 Kent St.; Tel.: (613) 238-1122 /1-800-333-3333.

Ramada Hotel (104/L29)
Quiet facility on corner close to Parliament Hill. Studio, one and two bedroom suites, fitness centre. Good for families.
233 rooms; 111 Cooper St.; Tel. (613) 238-1331 or 1-800-267-8378.

Sheraton Ottawa **(104/L28)**
★ Family-friendly hotel in central location with in-room movies, Nintendo, indoor pool and fitness centre.
236 rooms; 150 Albert St.; Tel. (613) 238-1500 or 1-800-489-8333.

The Westin **(104/L30)**
★✼ Stunning views and contemporary comforts in a plum but very pricey setting. The Westin is a favourite among business travellers. It has the city's largest ballroom. Connected to Rideau Centre shopping mall and city conference centre.
484 rooms; 11 Colonel By Drive; Tel: (613) 560-7000.

GROUP B HOTELS

Under $100 per night

Auberge McGee's Inn **(105/L30)**
Victorian mansion built in 1886 by John J. McGee, First Clerk of the Privy Council of Canada. Jacuzzis, fireplaces, dataports etc.
14 rooms; 185 Daly Ave.; Tel.: (613) 237-6089 or 1-800-2MCGEES.

Capital Hill Hotel & Suites **(100/K29)**
Modern and comfortable in central location three blocks from Parliament. Fitness centre.
150 rooms; 88 Albert St.; Tel. (613) 235-1413 or 1-800-463-7705.

Doral Inn **(100/K29)**
Quaint Victorian-style hotel located downtown. Lovely guest rooms and apartments, parlour with fireplace, nearby pool and spa.
40 rooms; 486 Albert St.; Tel.: (613) 230-8055; 1-800-263-6725.

Gasthaus Switzerland Inn **(105/L30)**
★ Charming inn run with Swiss-style efficiency since 1985. Central location, deluxe suites, wonderful breakfast.
22 rooms; 89 Daly Ave.; Tel.: (613) 237-0335 or 1-888-663-0000.

Southway Inn **(104/L29)**
Bright and modern, 102 rooms in south Ottawa location. Family owned and operated. Three housekeeping units for families.
102 rooms; 2431 Bank St.; Tel.: (613) 737-0811 or 1-800-267-9704.

WelcomINNS **(0)**
Modern hotel close to downtown. Free parking, complimentary continental breakfast, fitness facility. Weekend and corporate rates.
109 rooms; 1220 Michael St.; Tel.: (613) 748-7800 or 1-800-387-4381.

BED & BREAKFAST

There are numerous bed and breakfast establishments, from modern homes to Victorian and Edwardian houses, with features like English gardens, vegetarian meals, etc. Most are small and intimate and priced in the $50 to $75 range.
For a list of fully-inspected homes, contact the Ottawa Bed & Breakfast Association, 18 Queen Elizabeth Dr.; Tel.: (613) 563-0161 or 1-800-461-7889.

Brighton House B&B **(0)**
★ Featured on the TV series,

"Best Places to Kiss." Gorgeous Edwardian 'sister' houses. Each suite is decorated in a different theme.
Six suites; $96-$129. 308 First Avenue; Tel: (613) 233-7777.

Regina Guest House   (102/C4)
Private rooms or hostel accommodation near Parliament Hill and National Art Gallery. *30 beds. $18-$44 per night. 205 Charlotte St.; Tel.: (613) 241-0908.*

Accommodations with ambience

Albert House Inn   (100/K29)
Gracious 1875 inn built by the Dominion of Canada's chief architect, Thomas Seaton Scot. Former head office for Victorian Order of Nurses, a convent, a flophouse and later abandoned before restoration. 17 rooms decorated in Victorian style.
$72-$138. *478 Albert Street; Tel.: (613) 236-4479/1-800-267-1982.*

Carmichael Inn   (104/M29)
★ Luxurious treatments, such as hydrotherapy baths and herbal body wraps. Centrally located in a gorgeous 1901 heritage building. 11 rooms. From $134. Spa packages extra. *46 Cartier St.; Tel. (613) 236-4667.*

Chateau Laurier   (100/K29)
★ ❧ Grand 1907 hotel in French Renaissance style. Overlooks Ottawa River. Luxurious ballrooms, stately lobby; lounge features portraits by the photographer Karsh, who called the hotel home for 14 years. Has hosted numerous royals and celebrities. 426 suites and rooms. $179-$500; packages available. *1 Rideau Street; Tel. (613) 241-1414 or 1-800-441-1414.*

Lord Elgin Hotel   (100/K29)
★ Elegant 1941 downtown landmark with Norman-style copper turrets, spacious Italian marble lobby and attentive, efficient staff. 312 fully modernized rooms from $135. Across from Confederation Park and National Arts Centre. *100 Elgin St. at Laurier Ave.; Tel. (613) 235-3333 or 1-800-267-4298.*

Ottawa Intl. Hostel   (104/L30)
★ For a little something different! Great location and atmosphere in the former Carleton County Jail. 150 beds. $21-$50. Book ahead for private rooms.
75 Nicholas St.; Tel. (613) 235-2595.

Paterson House   (105/L30)
Executive bed and breakfast in beautifully restored 1901 Queen Anne mansion, former home of Senator Norman Paterson. Offers Maharishi Panchakarma treatments to soothe and relax the body and soul. Four large, luxurious suites and conference facilities. $135-$195. Treatments extra. *500 Wilbrod Street; (613) 565-8996.*

Festivals, flowers and fireworks

The city's activity calendar is full year round.

The nation's capital is so much more than stodgy politicians and governmental affairs. Ottawa bursts with excitement and colour throughout the year. The diverse seasons provide a fitting backdrop for every occasion. Spring explodes with colour during the annual Tulip Festival. Warm summer air carries the sights and sounds of numerous celebrations, including a variety of music festivals. The autumn landscape is painted with brilliant colour as the leaves start to fall and the hot air balloons rise. Even when the weather is at its frostiest, Ottawa celebrates with fun and games during Winterlude.

PUBLIC HOLIDAYS

On most of the following days, post offices, schools, some stores and most offices are closed:
1 January *(New Year's Day)*

Fireworks light up the night sky in spectacular fashion during Winterlude in February.

Good Friday & Easter Monday
Monday before May 25 *(Victoria Day)*
1 July *(Canada Day)*
First Monday in August *(Civic holiday)*
First Monday in September *(Labour Day)*
2nd Monday in October *(Thanksgiving)*
11 November *(Remembrance Day)*
25 December *(Christmas)*
26 December *(Boxing Day)*

SPECIAL EVENTS

For further details regarding exact location and prices, please contact the Capital Infocentre at 1-800-465-1867 or (613) 239-5000. Or call the phone number provided for each event.

February

Three weekends in February:
Winterlude/Bal de Neige
Winter isn't a time to sit inside when you're visiting the Capital. Get out and prove you're made of hearty stock. Skate the Rideau Canal, the world's longest skating

MARCO POLO SELECTION: EVENTS

1 Canada Day
The best birthday bash in
the country (page 73)

2 Winterlude
Skating, events, ice and
snow sculptures warm up
February (page 71)

3 Canadian Tulip Festival
The city is ablaze with
floral beauty and fun
(page 72)

**4 Gatineau Hot Air
Balloon Festival**
The skies are alive with
brilliant colour each fall
(page 74)

5 Bluesfest
Hot licks and cool tunes
make this one marvellous
musical fest (page 73)

6 Ottawa Intl. Jazz Festival
Sensational sounds from
the world's top jazz
musicians (page 74)

7 Festival Franco-Ontarien
Plenty of activities and
joie de vivre (page 73)

8 Italian Week Festival
Great food, festivities and
fun celebrating Italian
culture (page 72)

rink! Watch sculptors make
magic with ice and snow. Visit
Snowflake Kingdom.

May

Mid-May: *Canadian Tulip
Festival*. A rainbow of three
million tulips beautify Canada's
Capital each year, representing
Holland's gratitude to our
nation's efforts during wartime.
Celebrations include concerts,
craft shows, and a flotilla of boats
on the Rideau Canal.
Tel. (613) 567-5757.

Last weekend in May: *National
Capital Air Show*. Look to the
skies for a spectacular show.
*Macdonald-Cartier International
Airport. Tel. (613) 526-1030.*

End of May: *Odawa Pow Wow*.
Witness tradition as native
culture comes alive with drums,
dance, arts and crafts. *Ottawa-
Nepean Tent and Trailer Park; Tel.*

(613) 722-3811.

June

First week in June: *Children's
Festival de la Jeunesse*. Magic.
Jugglers. Clowns. Stories.
Crafts. It all adds up to fun.
*Canadian Museum of Nature; Tel.
(613) 728-5863.*

Mid-June: *Italian Week Festival*.
The Italian community parties
with panache — and you're
invited. Enjoy music, art, a
soccer tournament, and of
course, great food. *Preston Street;
(613) 729-9518.*

Last two weekends of June:
Ottawa Fringe Festival. Creativity
throbs throughout this festival
that showcases independent
theatre, dance, music, visual art
and more. *Arts Court; Tel. (613)
232-6162.*

End of June: *National Capital
Dragon Boat Race Festival*. This

free event features the unique sport of dragon boat racing, as well as activities and entertainment for kids and adults. *Mooney's Bay; Tel. (613) 238-7711.*

End of June: *Festival Franco-Ontarien.* French Canadians know how to party. Come celebrate the vibrant culture with music, art, kids' shows and more. *Tel. (613) 788-0999 or (613) 741-1225.*

July

★ July 1: *Canada Day.* Celebrate Canada's biggest birthday party on Capital Hill. The whole family is invited to enjoy the concerts, excitement and the best fireworks display in the country. *Parliament Hill.*

Early July: *Ottawa Citizen Bluesfest.* Ain't got no destination? Catch the finest musicians to sing the blues at the biggest festival of its kind in Canada. *Tel. (613) 233-8798.*

Early July: *H.O.P.E. Beach Volleyball Tournament.* The largest beach volleyball tournament in the world attracts noteworthy musicians, 1,000 teams and thousands of spectators. The end result is monetary donations to over 70 charities. *Tel. (613) 237-1433.*

Early-mid-July: *Pride Festival.* Celebrate the diversity of the lesbian and gay community at the

Costumed characters add good-natured fun to Winterlude celebrations.

The Central Canada Exhibition has midway rides, exhibits and more.

Pride Day Parade, Rainbow Party and community fair. *Tel. (613) 238-2424.*

Mid-end of July: *Ottawa International Jazz Festival.* Ten days of jazz. If that sounds sweet, make sure you catch the world's finest musicians in this heppest of celebrations. *Tel. (613) 241-2633.*

Late July-early August: *Ottawa Chamber Music Festival.* North America's largest chamber music festival is brought to some of the most beautiful churches in downtown Ottawa. Winner of the Lieutenant Governor's Award for the Arts in '96, '97 and '98. *Ottawa churches. Tel. (613) 234-8008 or 1-800-267-8378.*

August

Mid-August: *Fete Caribe.* Join the party as the annual Caribbean festival leaves a trail of colour and joy during the parade, boat cruise, and concert. There are kids' activities and arts & crafts too. *Various downtown locations. Tel. (613) 739-0070.*

Mid-late August: *Central Canada Exhibition.* The 11-day exhibition has something for everyone: midway, pavilions, entertainment, outdoor shows. *Lansdowne Park; (613) 237-7222.*

Last weekend in August: *CKCU Ottawa Folk Festival.* Be part of Canada's folk tradition. *Tel. (613) 230-8234.*

September

Early September: *Gatineau Hot Air Balloon Festival.* Look! Up in the air! The Ottawa skyline is dotted with brilliance, beauty and novelty as over 100 hot air balloons from various countries tour the heavens. On the ground are shows, activities and midway rides. *La Baie Parc, Gatineau; Tel. (819) 243-2330 or 1-800-668-8383.*

Mid-Late September: *Making Scenes Film and Video Festival.* Independent films and videos by Canadian and international film-makers. *Tel. (613) 566-2113 or 1-877-566-2113.*

Mid-September-Mid-October: *Fall Rhapsody.* To truly appreciate the beauty of autumn, take part in this outdoor event that includes activities and fun for the whole family. *Gatineau Park (819) 827-2020 or 1-800-465-1867.*

Autumn (Dates vary): *Ottawa International Animation Festival.* Creative types, executives, students and film lovers from around the world converge at the world's second largest animation festival. *Tel. (613) 232-8769.*

December

December-early January: *Christmas Lights Across Canada.* Bright lights perk up the

Canada Day fireworks with the Peace Tower in the foreground.

nation's capital during the festive season. This powerful display of unity and good cheer is a must-see along *Confederation Boulevard and Parliament Hill.*

A Gift of Colour, Friendship and Life

During the Second World War, Holland's royal family found sanctuary in Ottawa. While in exile, Princess Juliana — heir to the Dutch throne — gave birth to a girl (Princess Margriet) at Ottawa Civic Hospital. The maternity room had to be declared Dutch soil for the event, and a Dutch flag flew from the Peace Tower to celebrate. At the end of the war, Canadian troops liberated the Netherlands from German occupation. Seven thousand Canadian soldiers died, while the survivors helped to rebuild the broken homes and dykes. In 1945, the Netherlands sent thousands of tulip bulbs to thank Canadians for their part in the liberation. This beautiful tradition of colour and life continues every spring.

After five

Forget the image cast by the suits of Parliament
— Ottawa residents know how to unwind after work.

The heart of the nation beats to a variety of rhythms. Classical, rock, jazz and blues emanate from clubs, pubs, and concert halls. Just follow the sound that stirs your soul. Ottawa's cultural events are world-class. Dance, theatre, opera and ballet are on the agenda year-round. For those who like to shout back at the entertainment, there's always hockey or baseball. And, if you're feeling lucky, the Casino de Hull awaits.

It is impossible to list the numerous options you have during your stay. For comprehensive listings of what's out there – perm-anently and during limited runs – pick up a free copy of *Where* or *Xpress*. Ottawa's daily newspaper, *The Ottawa Citizen,* is also a good resource, as is the *Ottawa Tourism Calendar of Events,* available at the tourism office at 130 Albert Street.

Bars and clubs close at

Street performers enliven the Ottawa street scene in summer.

2am in Ottawa. Those who love to party into the wee hours can journey across the river to Hull, Quebec where nightspots are open until 3am.

CASINO

Casino de Hull   (100/G28)
★ Gaming tables and slot machines await you in this glittering adult world. Also two restaurants, one snack bar and two bars. It's a gambler's heaven in Hull.
Open: 11am - 3am Group packages available. Leamy Lake (Take Macdonald-Cartier Bridge north from Ottawa to the Boulevard du Casino exit) Tel. (819) 772-2100.

COMEDY

Yuk Yuk's Komedy Kabaret   (100/K29)
Did you hear the one about the best place to catch great stand-up? Well, a guy (or gal) walks

MARCO POLO SELECTION: ENTERTAINMENT

1 National Arts Centre
Canada's premiere showcase for the performing arts (page 78)

2 Casino de Hull
Games of chance, gourmet restaurants, world-class entertainment (page 77)

3 The Rainbow Bistro
Live blues and jazz every day and night (page 80)

4 Zaphod Beeblebrox
Eclectic bands in a communal atmosphere (page 80)

5 Barrymore's
Live music in a renovated theatre (page 80)

6 Great Canadian Theatre Company
Award-winning Canadian theatre (page 83)

7 Corel Centre
Home of pro hockey and big name concerts (page 78)

8 The Cave
Dance club with cigar lounge and martini bar (page 79)

9 Ottawa Little Theatre
Put a little drama or comedy in your life (page 83)

10 Liquor Dome
Ottawa's largest dance club with six bars on two levels (page 79)

into a club, takes a seat and yuks it up all evening. Wednesdays-Saturdays. *88 Albert St. (Capital Hill Hotel) (613) 236-5233. Cover charge.*

CONCERTS

Corel Centre **(0)**
★ Home of the Ottawa Senators hockey team, it also hosts great concerts and other entertainment.
For upcoming event info, call (613) 599-0100; 1000 Palladium Drive, Kanata. www.corelcentre.com

Lansdowne Park **(104/N29)**
Concerts, sporting events, trade shows and more.

1015 Bank St. Tel. (613) 564-1485.

National Arts Centre **(100/K29)**
★ The stage of this arena has been graced by a diverse variety of shows, including Canadian and international musicals, theatre and dance performances.
For information about what's coming up, call (613) 996-5051. 53 Elgin St. www.nac-cna.ca

Opera Lyra Ottawa **(105/L30)**
Powerful voice and emotion spill from the stage as drama and passion unfold. Operates year round.
110-2 Daly Ave. (613) 233-9200.

DANCE CLUBS

The Cave (104/L29)
★ The club that likes to mix it up. Different themes and musical styles each night. Cigar lounge and martini bar too. *Cover charge most nights. 63 Bank St.; Tel. (613) 233-0080.*

The Factory (100/K30)
150,000 watts of sound and light. Pool tables, two dance floors, six bars and two lounges. *Wed.-Sat. Cover charge most nights. 160 Rideau & Dalhousie St.; Tel. (613) 241-6869. www.thefactory.ca*

Houlihan's (100/K30)
♣ Sweat it out on the dance floor Thursday to Sunday. *Cover charge. 110 York St.; Tel. (613) 241-5455.*

Illusion (100/K30)
Dance club for the 30-something crowd. Dress code in effect. Lounge in back with couches and candlelight. Theme nights. *Thurs.-Mon. 9:30pm-2am 283 Dalhousie Street; Tel. (613) 789-9995.*

Le Bistro (100/J28)
♣ On the Quebec side of the border, party to pop and rock tunes in this chic two-level club. *No cover charge. 3 Kent St., Hull; Tel. (819) 778-0968.*

Le Bop Bar (100/J28)
You don't have to be under 25 to feel like part of the cool crowd here. Wide range of dance music. *Cover charge some nights. Aubry, Hull; Tel. (819) 777-3700.*

Liquor Dome (100/K30)
★ ♣ Room for up to 1,000 in Ottawa's largest warehouse-style dance club. Six bars on two levels, four pool tables, foosball table. *Cover charge some nights. 200 Rideau St. (at Cumberland); Tel. (613) 562-2512.*

Maxwell's Bistro (104/L29)
Popular club with dance music Thursdays, Fridays and Saturdays. Karaoke Tuesdays. Lounge singer Johnny Vegas croons on Wednesdays. *No cover. 340 Elgin St.; Tel. (613) 232-5771.*

Reactor (100/K30)
♣ ❀ Club for the 19 to 25 set, with dancing, pool tables, two bars. Top 40 hits. *18 York Street; Tel. (613) 241-8955.*

Stoney's (100/K30)
❀ ♣ Huge outside patio is filled with the young crowd on summer nights. During cool weather, dance in the club or catch sports on the big screen. *62 York St.; Tel. (613) 241-8858; no cover charge.*

LIVE MUSIC

After Eight Jazz Club (104/L29)
So cool, it's hot. Live jazz Thursday to Saturday. Most shows start at 9 and at 11pm. *Cover charge. Main entrance Metcalfe & Wellington St.; Tel. (613) 237-5200.*

Barrymore's (104/L29)

★ And now, our feature presentation: Canadian and international bands - mostly rock - take to the stage in this renovated movie theatre.

Doors open at 8pm, most shows start at 9. Cover charge. 323 Bank St.; Tel. (613) 233-0307.

Cajun Attic (101/K30)

Upstairs, get into the live blues and rock bands performing Thursday to Saturday.
594 Rideau St.; Tel. (613) 789-1185.

Perfect Strangers (100/K30)

Specializing in live entertainment: blues, rock, reggae, stand-up and improv comedy.
Cover charge. 211 Rideau St.; Tel. (613) 241-2255.

The Rainbow Bistro (100/K30)

★❀ The quintessential blues club. Live blues day (4-7pm) and night (9:30pm-2am) seven days a week.
Cover charge some days. 76 Murray St. (upstairs); Tel. (613) 241-5123.

Tucson's Roadhouse (104/L29)

Would you like an order of blues with your dinner? Live entertainment Fridays and Saturdays.
Cover charge. 2440 Bank St.; Tel. (613) 738-7596.

Zaphod Beeblebrox (100/K30)

★♨ You don't have to pronounce it. Just get into it as eclectic bands move the room.
Cover charge most nights. Two locations: 27 York St., (613) 562-1010; 363 Bank St.; (613) 594-3355; www.zaphodbeeblebrox.com

Zuma's Texas Grill & Dance Hall (0)

For country music lovers, this popular hot spot has live music, DJ and line dancing.
Cover charge. 1211 Lemieux Street (corner of St. Laurent Blvd. and Highway 417), Gloucester. Tel. (613) 742-9378.

LOUNGES/PIANO BARS

Franky's on Frank (104/M28)

A gay bar/lounge in an elegant 19th century mansion. Live shows Wed.-Sun.
Cover charge. 303 Frank St.; Tel. (613) 233-9195.

Friday's Roast Beef House (104/L29)

In the mood for a melody? Let the piano man entertain from 8:30 p.m.
No cover. 150 Elgin St.; Tel. (613) 237-5353.

Full House Parlour (104/L29)

Ladies' night Tuesday. Live piano Monday to Saturday.
No cover. 337 Somerset St. W. (at Bank); Tel. (613) 238-6734.

Vineyards Wine Bar Bistro (100/K30)

Appropriately located in a cellar, Vineyards is an award winning wine bar that serves bistro fare. Live jazz Wednesday and Sunday evenings.
No cover charge. 54 York St. (cellar of York & William); Tel. (613) 241-4270.

MOVIES

A number of multiplex theatres

run first-run films. Complete listings are in newspapers *Xpress* and *The Ottawa Citizen*. For cheaper flicks and cult classics, check out *Mayfair Theatre (1074 Bank Street)*, which features two films for the price of one. For foreign films, visit *The Bytowne (325 Rideau Street)*, an alternative cinema and repertory house. If you like big screens, *Imax/Omnimax* is at *The Canadian Museum of Civilization, 100 rue Laurier, Hull. For comprehensive listings, log on at http://movies.ottawa.com*

PUBS

D'Arcy McGee's   (100/K29)

Named after one of Confederation's founding fathers who was shot and killed in 1868 just a few steps from where the pub now stands. Designed and handcrafted in Ireland, the warm wood and glass interior provides a fitting backdrop for live Celtic and Maritime music Wed.- Sat.
44 Sparks St.; Tel. (613) 230-4433.

Earl of Sussex   (100/K29)

Authentic British pub gives you 27 choices of draft beer on tap. Live entertainment on Friday and Saturday.
431 Sussex Dr.; Tel. (613) 562-5544.

Fox and Feather   (100/K29)

Choose from 14 draft on tap, play some pool or try your skill at the dart board.
283 Elgin St.; Tel. (613) 233-2219.

Heart & Crown   (100/K29)

❀ Irish-owned pub with fun atmosphere has Celtic music Wednesday to Saturday nights. Private booths in The Snug Pub at the back for those who want more intimate surroundings. Big screen TV.
67 Clarence St.; Tel. (613) 562-0674.

Mad Cow Pub   (104/L29)

Things get lively Wednesday to Sunday nights with live folk music. Bring your voice and an instrument on Wednesday nights and bask in the spotlight
1070 Bank St. Tel. (613) 730-1020.

Lord Stanley and his Cup

That most holiest of Canadian grails – the Stanley Cup – was born in Ottawa . In 1892, Lord Stanley Preston, Canada's Governor General, was one of the original devoted hockey fans. He asked the best silversmith in London, England to make a gold-lined silver bowl on an ebony base to reward the best hockey team. The cost was ten guinea, or $48.67. Little did Lord Stanley know that he was also creating a legacy of players – and a legion of armchair fans – who would dream of hoisting his coveted cup.

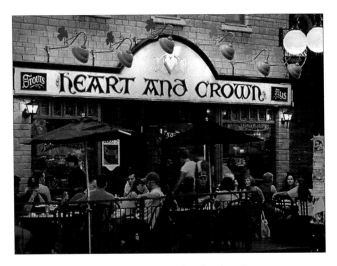

The popular Heart and Crown is a British-style pub in Ottawa

The Manx Pub (104/L29)

For your ears, folk music every Sunday and Monday evening. For your eyes, fine art displays adorn the pub walls every month.

370 Elgin St.; Tel. (613) 231-2070.

Mayflower II Pub & Restaurant (104/L29)

Comfortable pub with a great selection of beer and single malt Scotch.

Two locations: 247 Elgin St. (at Cooper); Tel. 238-3731; 201 Queen St.; Tel. (613) 238-1138.

Minglewood's (100/K30)

Three floors to keep you busy. A sports bar. Billiards and big screen TV. And a dance floor.

101 York St.; Tel. (613) 562-2611.

Molly McGuire's (100/K30)

Experience a wee bit of Ireland Wednesday through Saturday nights when live music fills the pub.

130 George St. (ByWard Market); Tel. (613) 241-1972.

Newfoundland Pub (105/L32)

Musicians pick up a fiddle and perform live tunes Fridays and Saturdays.

940a Montreal Rd.; Tel. (613) 745-0962.

RACETRACKS

Enjoy a day — or an evening — at the races. Watch harness horses vie to be first over the finish line. Group packages available. Call for race nights and special events. Live entertainment and fine dining too.

*Rideau Carleton Raceways
4837 Albion Road, Gloucester; 20 minutes from downtown. Tel. (613) 822-2211.*

SPORTS

Baseball (0)
Ottawa Lynx Baseball Club
Watch a first-rate team at affordable prices. The Triple-A affiliate team of the Montreal Expos plays at the 10,000-plus seat JetForm Park. Restaurant, luxury suites and a picnic area. *April-Sept.; $6.50-$8.50. 300 Coventry Rd.; Tel. (613) 749-9947 or 1-800-663-0985; www.ottawalynx.com.*

Hockey (0)
Watch the Ottawa Senators take on the rest of the National Hockey League teams at the Corel Centre, and get caught up in the passion of the nation's favourite sport.
Sept.-May $19-$125. 1000 Palladium Drive, Kanata. Tel. (613) 599-0300 or 1-800-444-SENS; www.corelcentre.co

SPORTS BARS

Tommy's Rooftop (102/P23)
Big screen TVs. Pool tables. Rooftop patio. Good food. *1280 Baseline Road; Tel. (613) 723-3300.*

STOCK CAR RACING

Capital City Speedway (0)
Catch the excitement of stock car racing. Free for kids. Licensed beverage area. Events from May-October.
7259 Hwy 7, Stittsville; 836-1807.

THEATRE

Great Canadian Theatre Company (104/L28)
★ The intimate setting of this playhouse features award-winning Canadian theatre.
910 Gladstone Ave.; Tel. (613) 236-5196. www.gctc.ca

Odyssey Theatre (101/K31)
Even actors like to play outside in summer. Open air theatre on the banks of the Rideau River in Strathcona Park.
Range Road and Laurier Ave. E.; Tel. (613) 232-8407.

Ottawa Little Theatre (101/K31)
★ Little theatre offers big entertainment: a play a month at not-so-big prices.
400 King Edward Ave.; Tel. (613) 233-8948.

The Right to Bear Art

Canadian dignitaries have security people, but to a lesser degree than their American counterparts. This was never more evident than when an intruder broke into Prime Minister Jean Chretien's residence in 1996. Guards, who thought an animal had jumped the fence, didn't react. The intruder got as far as the Prime Minister's bedroom. Chretien, who heard a noise in the hallway, armed himself with an Inuit carving. His wife, Aline, called police. Since then, security has been beefed up at 24 Sussex, but our politicians have always been more approachable.

Strolling the Capital

Exploring Ottawa's proud history on foot makes for a fascinating few hours.

① DISCOVER THE HILL

Parliament Hill stands as a national landmark and the centre stage of political life in Canada. The Parliament Buildings consist of: the Centre Block, built between 1916 and 1920, home of the House of Commons and the Senate, where laws are debated and passed; the East Block, constructed between 1859 and 1865, containing senators' offices and rooms recreated in Confederation-era style; and the West Block, constructed between 1859 and 1865, which houses offices of ministers and members of Parliament. You can pick up a Discover the Hill tour booklet at the Capital Infocentre. This tour is approximately 45 minutes.

Start your tour at *Queen Victoria's statue* behind the West Block. The statue, unveiled in 1901, honours the monarch who chose Ottawa as the capital of Canada in 1857, which at that time consisted of Ontario and Quebec. Slightly west is *Lester B. Pearson's* monument; the 14th prime minister originated the concept of UN Peacekeeping forces. Share his "chair" and you should be able to spot at least a dozen Canadian flags. In 1965, Pearson rallied support for the uniquely Canadian flag you see today.

Head east along the riverbank to the *Noon-Day Gun,* donated by the British Army in 1854 to its Canadian garrison. The two-ton muzzle-loading ship's cannon was used during the Crimean war. It was purchased by the postal minister in 1869 and was fired at noon to allow postal employees to synchronize their watches, regulating the quality of the postal service.

Beside the Noon-Day Gun, you'll find an unlikely attraction: the *"cat sanctuary"* which has been home to stray cats since the 1970s. For years, senior citizen Rene Chartrand has been self-appointed guardian to the cat colony, which also includes raccoons, squirrels, chickadees, sparrows and more. He ensures that the menagerie is fed and that the whimsical shelters of the cats are maintained.

Continue east along the river walk and you'll see the statue of *Sir George-Étienne Cartier,* one of the Fathers of Confederation. His statue, unveiled in 1885, was the first monument erected on Parliament Hill. His statue and that of *Sir John A. Macdonald's* are in perfect symmetry in relation to the Centre Block, in honour of the two political allies' long friendship.

Two other statues in close proximity honour *Alexander Mackenzie,* prime minister from 1873 to 1878, who gave Canadians the right to a secret ballot; and *George Brown,* who helped form the Great Coalition of the 1860s, which brought about Confederation. Follow the scenic *"Lovers' Walk"* along the shoreline of the Ottawa River to the *Summer Pavilion* for a spectacular view of the Gatineau Hills, the Ottawa River and Chaudiere Falls. The pavilion, rebuilt in 1995 thanks to the contribution of the Canadian Police Association, pays tribute to men and women killed while performing their duties as police and peace officers.

Next you'll encounter *Thomas D'Arcy McGee's* statue. McGee, a Father of Confederation, was known for his powerful speeches and was referred to as the first Canadian Nationalist.

It's impossible not to notice the Library of Parliament, one of the best examples of Gothic Revival architecture in Canada. The magnificent circular 1876 building survived the fire of 1916 which destroyed the original Centre Block.

Head east to the statues depicting *Robert Baldwin and Sir Louis-Hippolyte Lafontaine,* architects of the principle of responsible government adopted by Canada in 1848.

Turn west and look for *Queen Elizabeth II's statue.* The British monarch, who has reigned since 1952, is astride one of her beloved horses. Close to the queen you'll find Sir John A. Macdonald's monument. Canada's first prime minister shaped the country's history through his leadership as a Father of Confederation and through his vision of a united country from ocean to ocean.

Swing south toward the East Block and you'll encounter the statue depicting *William Lyon Mackenzie King,* who held power for nearly 22 years, a record for all prime ministers. He introduced the country's first social programs such as the Canada Pension Plan and Unemployment Insurance and also introduced Canadian citizenship.

Walk to the front of the East Block and turn east and you'll see *Sir Wilfrid Laurier's statue.* He was the first francophone prime minister of Canada, from 1896 to 1911.

The East Block houses the Prime Minister's office and those of many senators. The East Block also boasts many strange animal forms on its buildings, known as "grotesques", which are common features in neo-gothic architecture.

Swing west along the front of the Centre Block to the *Centennial Flame.* It's fueled by Alberta natural gas and is the symbolic torch lighting the way for the second century of Confederation.

The Centre Block's most striking feature is the *Peace Tower,* a bell tower built from 1919 to 1927 to commemorate the 60,000 plus Canadians who died in the first World War. Inside the tower are 53 bells of the carillon, a set of tuned bells which can be heard throughout the city.

Conclude your tour of Parliament Hill with two statues near the West Block: *John Diefenbaker's* monument to the rear of the block, which honours the man who brought us the Canadian Bill of Rights; and at the front of the West Block, S*ir Robert Borden,* who led the country during the First World War, and in 1918, passed an act giving female British subjects over the age of 18 the right to vote.

② CONFEDERATION BLVD. SOUTH

This 35 minute tour highlights some of the exceptional public art created by Canadians from across the country. For more art tours, pick up the Street SmART booklet at the Capital Infocentre or call (613) 239-5000 or 1-800-465-1867.

Start your tour at *The Museum of Contemporary Photography,* a former railway station, at Elgin and Wellington Streets. Cross the street to admire *The Response,* the National War Memorial. The 23 bronze figures represent the various services involved in World War I. The figures moving through the arch symbolize the emergence from war to peace, while the winged figures above symbolize peace and liberty.

Just slightly south on Elgin Street at the National Arts Centre, you'll find the popular sculpture, *Balancing,* by artist John Hooper. The playful piece depicts a cross section of residents, including a bemused bureaucrat. You'll also spot Terres des hommes, first exhibited at Expo 67, by Suzanne Guité.

Continue south on Elgin to Confederation Park, directly across from the historic Lord Elgin Hotel. Here you will find several monuments, including the 1888 Northwest Rebellion, commemorating two members of the Sharpshooters' Company of the Governor General's Foot Guards: Privates John Rogers and William Osgoode, who died at the Battle of Cutknife Hill in 1885 during the Riel Rebellion.

The park's lovely fountain stood in *Trafalgar Square* in London, England from 1845 to 1955 and is named the Colonel By Fountain in honour of Bytown's founder.

The Polish Home Army Tribute, by T. Slesicki in 1964, commemorates 26 Canadian airmen who died in Poland during the Second World War. The nearby 1902 Boer War Memorial was funded by the pennies collected by 30,000 school children and honours Canadian volunteers who died in South Africa early in the century. It's believed the model for sculpture was the son of sculptor Hamilton MacCarthy.

Also in Confederation Park, look for the **Kwakiutl Totem** created by native artist Henry Hunt in 1971. It was donated by the province of British Columbia and marks the centennial of that province's entry into Canada. Similar totems were donated at the same time to other territories and provinces.

Head south on Elgin Street to Nepean Street. There you will find the *Canadian Tribute to Human Rights,* honouring the struggles and continuing efforts of the people of Canada and all nations to obtain and preserve fundamental human rights. A group of private citizens raised funds nationally from individuals, associations and businesses to fund the piece, which was created by Montreal artist Melvin Charney in 1989 and unveiled in 1990 by exiled Tibetan Buddhist leader, the Dalai Lama.

③ MILE OF HISTORY

This short tour acquaints you with several of the city's best-known historic and cultural attractions.

Begin at Sussex and Rideau Streets, across from Chapters bookstore. Cross Rideau Street and continue west on Sussex Drive. You'll pass the historic Chateau Laurier Hotel and the Canadian Museum of Contemporary Photography and will have an excellent view of the Bytown Locks.

Return to the corner of Rideau and Sussex and make a left-hand turn on Mackenzie Street. It will take you past the monolithic American Embassy and on the left is Major's Hill Park, site of many festivals. As you walk north, you'll see the Peacekeeping Monument and the stunning National Gallery of Canada. Stroll past it to Alexandra Bridge for a beautiful view of the Ottawa River.

Across from the gallery is Ottawa's oldest church, the Notre-Dame Cathedral Basilica, and farther north on Sussex is the Royal Canadian Mint and Canadian War Museum.

Walking back along the east side of Sussex, look for "The Angel" at the corner of St. Patrick Street. Turn left onto Murray Street and immediately right and you'll find yourself in the ByWard Market and in a courtyard called Tin House Court where the cobblestones and unique architecture will make you think you've stepped back in time.

Practical information

Useful addresses, information and survival tips

BILINGUAL CULTURE

Since Ottawa is the nation's capital, and a mere stone's throw from Quebec – Canada's Francophone province – many residents speak French as well as English. You will easily get by using solely English, but if you ask "Ou est la museum?", most people will understand.

CAR RENTAL

Book cars or campers well in advance at your travel bureau. This is much cheaper and safer than trying to arrange for transportation after you arrive. It is advisable to return your vehicle to your starting point as there are often extremely high return charges should you attempt to return it at an affiliate.

CULTURAL INFORMATION

Information on cultural events such as plays, concerts, movies, sporting events, etc. can be found in a variety of magazines and newspapers distributed throughout the city: *Where,* free monthly magazine; *Capital Express,* free weekly newspaper; *Today's Seniors,* a free paper for older adults; *Capital Parent,* geared to families; *The Ottawa Citizen* daily newspaper; and the *Ottawa Tourism Calendar of Events* which can be picked up only at the tourism office at 130 Albert Street.

CUSTOMS

Visitors to Canada should note that firearms are not permitted. Restrictions are placed upon fruits and vegetables, meat, plants and animals. If you're over the age of 19, you may bring in free of duty up to 200 cigarettes, 50 cigars, 200 tobacco sticks and 200 grams of loose tobacco. Regarding alcohol, you can bring 1.14 litres (40 oz.) of wine or liquor, or twenty-four 355 ml (12 oz.) cans of beer or ale. For more information, call (905) 612-7937 or contact www.rc.gc.ca.
Returning U.S. citizens who spend more than 48 hours in

Canada may bring back U.S. $400 worth of goods duty-free. This exemption may only apply every 30 days. Goods can include 100 cigars or 200 cigarettes (Cuban tobacco excepted), as well as one litre of wine, beer or liquor, if you are at least 21-years-old. If you have more than $1,000 (plus the duty-free exemption) of goods, you must itemize all purchases on the back of the declaration form, so please retain your sales slips and invoices. Canada has restrictions in place to keep objects that are of historical, cultural or scientific significance in Canada.

In Ontario, drivers are permitted to turn right on a red light as long as they yield for the green light traffic. Speed limit signs are clearly marked, and are recorded in kilometres. You are not allowed to pass school buses when their warning lights are flashing – even if you are going in the opposite direction. The Canadian Automobile Association (CAA) is always prepared to help members of other automobile associations (take your membership card along).

Metric System

1 kilometre = .621 miles
(Don't speed. 100 kph = 60 mph)

1 centimetre = .3937 inches
(Inchworm is easier to say than 2.54-centimetre-worm)

1 millilitre = .034 fluid ounces
(A 355 mL soft drink = about 12 ounces)

1 kilogram = 2.204 pounds
(A 130-pound person weighs 59 kgs.)

1 litre = 1.057 quarts
(A litre of milk is a little bigger than a quart of milk)

0 Celsius = 32 Fahrenheit (Multiply by 9, divide by 5, add 32)
(When it's -20C, you'll need your coat and toque. When it's +20C, it's time for shorts and a T-shirt).

ELECTRICITY

110 Volts at 60 Hertz. It is advisable for Europeans to buy a suitable adapter for hair dryers and electric razors.

EMBASSIES

Ambassade De France
42 Sussex Drive
Tel: (613) 789-1795

Embassy of the United States of America
100 Wellington
Tel: (613) 238-5335

Most embassies are located in Ottawa, but a few consulates, including the ones listed here, are in Toronto:
China (416) 964-7260
Italy (416) 977-1566
U.K. (416) 593-1267

FISHING

Before you decide to reel in a big one, you'll need a fishing license, which can be obtained in all sports stores or lodges for a fee of $10-$30. In national parks, a special fishing license is required.

LIQUOR LAWS

To purchase liquor, look for the government owned stores (The Beer Store and LCBO). If it's after hours, you can cross over to Hull to buy beer and wine in convenience stores, which are often open all night. The legal drinking age in Ontario is 19. Bars usually close at 2am in Ontario. If you feel like staying out later, closing time is 3am in Quebec.

MEDICAL ASSISTANCE

Dial 9-1-1 for emergency medical treatment. For less serious matters, go to a local clinic (look in the yellow pages under Clinics) or a hospital. Visiting a hospital can be extremely costly. British citizens are recommended to take out a one-year travel insurance policy, which covers common illnesses. American citizens should ensure that their health insurance policy covers them outside the U.S.

METRIC SYSTEM

Canada's highway signs are marked in kilometres, each of which is equivalent to .62 miles. Temperature is recorded in degrees Celsius. To convert Celsius into Fahrenheit, multiply by 9, divide by 5 and add 32 degrees. Food and beverages packaged in Canada are measured in grams and litres. While Canadians have been gently urged to employ the Metric system for years, there are many people – especially the older generation – who still understand (and use) the Imperial system.

MONEY

The Canadian wallet is weighed down with a multitude of coins. Of course, there's the penny, nickel, dime and quarter. But there is also the dollar (loonie) and the two-dollar coin (toonie).

Most purchases are made with debit cards or credit cards (MasterCard, Visa). However, make sure you have cash on hand to pay taxi drivers, porters, etc. Many stores, hotels and restaurants accept American money, but you can't always be assured that you are getting the current exchange rate.

Foreign currency can be exchanged at any bank or exchange house, including Custom House Currency Exchange, Canada's largest foreign currency broker.

Open Monday to Friday throughout the year, Saturday from May to September. Located one block south of Parliament Hill at 153 Sparks Street. Foreign currency can also be exchanged at most banks, including AMEX Bank of Canada at 360 Albert Street.

NEWS FROM HOME

For those who are feeling a little homesick, these shops stock many national and international newspapers and magazines.

Britton's Smoke Shop: *844 Bank Street, the Glebe; Tel: (613) 235-6826.*

Daily News Smokery Ltd.: *1980 Ogilvie Rd. (Gloucester Centre); (613) 748-6397.*

Globe Mags & Cigars: *57 William (ByWard Market); (613) 241-7274.*

Mags & Fags: *254 Elgin; (613) 233-9651.*

PASSPORTS

Permanent residents of the United States do not need a passport or any other immigration documents; only proof of identity (green card or birth certificate).

American citizens entering Canada from countries other than the U.S. need a valid passport, birth certificate or green card.

POLITICAL SATIRE

It's a sign of status − the first time − to be ridiculed in *Frank* magazine, the nation's satirical rag that targets politicians and other public figures. You'll find it at most newsstands.

POST OFFICES

Post offices are open Monday to Friday from 9am to 5pm and from 8am to noon on Saturdays. Stamps and postal services are usually offered in major drug stores. To mail a letter, look for the red Canada Post mailboxes. Letters and postcards mailed within Canada require 46-cent postage; to the U.S., it's 55-cents; and internationally, 95-cents.

SMOKING

Most restaurants and other public places are smoke-free, or have designated smoking areas.

TAXES

A sales tax of 7 per cent, known as GST, applies throughout Canada. In addition, there is provincial sales tax of 8 per cent. All taxes are added at the time of payment and not included on the menu or store price. Foreign visitors may apply for a refund of the GST.

metres; 10 cents for each additional metre.

TAXI FARES

If you hail a cab in the capital, fares are $2 for the first 85

TIME ZONE

Ottawa operates on Eastern Standard Time.

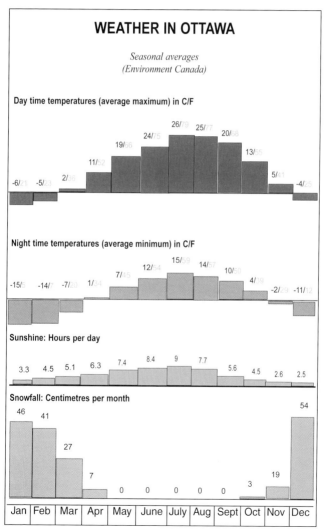

WEATHER IN OTTAWA

*Seasonal averages
(Environment Canada)*

Day time temperatures (average maximum) in C/F

-6/21 -5/23 2/36 11/52 19/66 24/75 26/79 25/77 20/68 13/55 5/41 -4/25

Night time temperatures (average minimum) in C/F

-15/5 -14/7 -7/20 1/34 7/45 12/54 15/59 14/57 10/50 4/19 -2/29 -11/12

Sunshine: Hours per day

3.3 4.5 5.1 6.3 7.4 8.4 9 7.7 5.6 4.5 2.6 2.5

Snowfall: Centimetres per month

46 41 27 7 0 0 0 0 0 3 19 54

| Jan | Feb | Mar | Apr | May | June | July | Aug | Sept | Oct | Nov | Dec |

TIPPING

Service charges are not included in restaurant bills. Many service occupation employees depend on tips to supplement their wages. Waiters should be tipped 15 per cent.; taxi drivers, 15 per cent; bell-hops, doormen and porters: $1 per item of luggage carried.

TOURIST INFORMATION

Start at the Capital Infocentre for information on sights to see, places to stay, and things to do. Whether you want to discover the impressive interiors of the museums, explore the city by bike, or get details about Parliament Hill, talk to the people who know the city best. Interactive displays and a 3D model of the city help you plan your itinerary.
Located across from Parliament Hill. 1-800-465-1867/(613) 239-5000; www.capcan.ca

A Mountie on Parliament Hill.

cities in Canada.

TRANSPORTATION

Getting around town often begins with a trip through the yellow pages. If you prefer to handle the wheel yourself, look under Automobile Renting. If you want someone else to do the driving, check out limousine and taxi services. The bus is also a reliable option, and OC Transpo offers a DayPass for unlimited travel all day on any city route. For fare and route information, call *(613) 741-4390*. To venture farther afield, several bus lines *(eg. Greyhound and Voyageur)* connect all major

WEATHER

The wardrobe of an Ottawa resident ranges from sandals to snowboots; cut-offs to parkas. The climate changes drastically from season to season. Summer can be pleasantly warm or uncomfortably sticky. Ottawa snowstorms are legendary for their ability to bury parked cars in a matter of hours. Autumn is magnificent as leaves turn vibrant red, yellow and orange. And in spring, residents are giddy as the masses of snow and ice melt and tulips bloom.

Do's and Don'ts

A few noteworthy tips for the unwary traveller

Ottawa is a very safe city to travel in. Still, you should always exercise care. When parking in a parking lot, don't leave your camera in the car where it can be seen, and don't walk down any dark side streets on your own at night.

Diamond lanes

The far right-hand lane of many busy streets is marked with diamond shapes. During certain hours of the day, stay out of these lanes: only buses and taxis may use them.

Firearms

Canadians are very strict about banning firearms. This is a very safe nation and the 'right to bear arms' is unnecessary.

Hotel parking

Parking is at a premium, therefore most hotels charge for the privilege.

Panhandlers

In recent years, there has been a rise in panhandlers and 'squeegee kids' in the capital. It is up to individuals whether to give them any money.

Parking

You may park on-street at parking meters and where permitted by signs. Where there are no signs regulating parking, you may park for a maximum three hours between 7am and 7pm Read the signs carefully before you park on-street. Many spots turn into No Stopping zones during rush hour.

Security

The need for extra security isn't as necessary in Canada's capital as it is in the United States, but if you'd like to see politicians in the House of Commons, you'll be scanned by metal detectors.

Smoking

Smoking is banned in public buildings and many restaurants (although some have smoking sections), even if you don't see a *No smoking* sign.

STREET ATLAS LEGEND

Legend *Légende*

Transportation
Transports

Expressway
Autoroute

Toll Expressway
Autoroute à péage

232 Exit Number
Numéro de sortie

Highway
Route provinciale

Scenic Parkway
Promenade pittoresque

Arterial Road
Artère principale

Collector Road
Rue collectrice

Local Road
Autre rue

Lane / Private Road
Ruelle / Rue privée

Road under construction
Rue en construction

Bus Terminal
Terminal d'autobus

One Way Street
Rue à sens unique

Railway
Chemin de fer

Rail Spur
Embranchement

Train Station
Gare de train

Services
Services

Fire Hall
Caserne de pompiers

Police Station
Poste de police

Hospital
Hôpital

Court House
Hôtel de Ville

Post Office
Bureau de poste

City or Town Hall
Hôtel de Ville

Travel Information
Renseignements touristiques

Boundaries
Limites

Municipal
Municipale

Regional
Régionale

International
Internationale

Water & Land
L'eau et la terre

Marina
Marina

Lake
Lac

River
Rivière

Streams
Ruisseaux

Marsh / Swamp
Ruisseaux

Intermittent Lake
Lac intermittent

Park
Parc

Parks Canada
Parcs Canada

Golf Course
Terrain de Golf

Cemetery
Cimetière

General Built-up
Cadre bâti

Attraction / Historic Site
Attrait / Lieu historique

Institution
Institution

Shopping Centre
Centre Commercial

Industrial
Zone industrielle

Quarry
Carrière

Building
Édifice

Culture
Culture

Place of Worship
Lieu religieux

Public Library
Bibliothèque

Live Theatre or Concert Hall
Théâtre ou Salle de concert

Museum or Art Gallery
Musée ou Galérie d'art

Cinema
Cinéma

Monument / Public Art
Monument / Art Public

Point of Interest
Point d'intérêt

Winery
Point d'intérêt

Recreation
Loisirs

Campground
Camping

Running Track
Piste

Outdoor Swimming Pool
Piscine extérieure

Indoor Swimming Pool
Piscine intérieure

Arena
Aréna

Outdoor Rink
Patinoire

Community Centre
Centre communataire

Race Track
Hippodrome

Bicycle Path
Voie cyclable

Walking Trail
Piste piétonnière

Education
Éducation

Public Elementary School
École publique élémentaire

Public Secondary School
École publique secondaire

Separate Elementary School
École catholique élémentaire

Separate Secondary School
École catholique secondaire

Private School
École privée

Commercial
Commercial

Liquor Store
Vins et spiritueux

Brewers Retail
Magasin des bières

Hotel/Motel
Hôtel/Motel

Road Designation
Classification routière

400 Ontario Provincial Hwy.
Rte. provinciale de l'Ontario

69 Ontario Regional Road
Route régionale de l'Ontario

96 Interstate Highway
Autoroute interstate

12 U.S. Highway
Route fédérale

384 New York State Highway
Route d'état New York

Getting around

Street atlas of the Nation's Capital

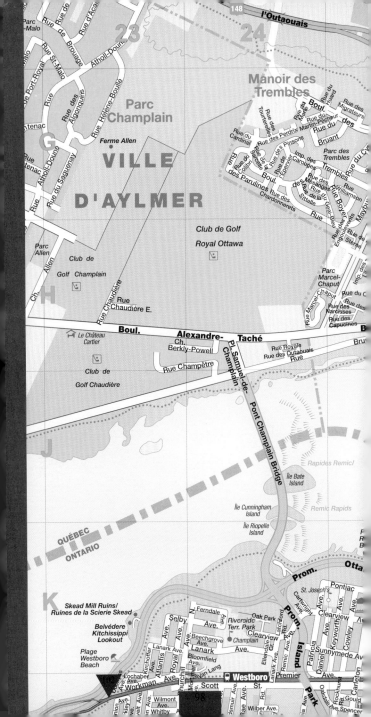

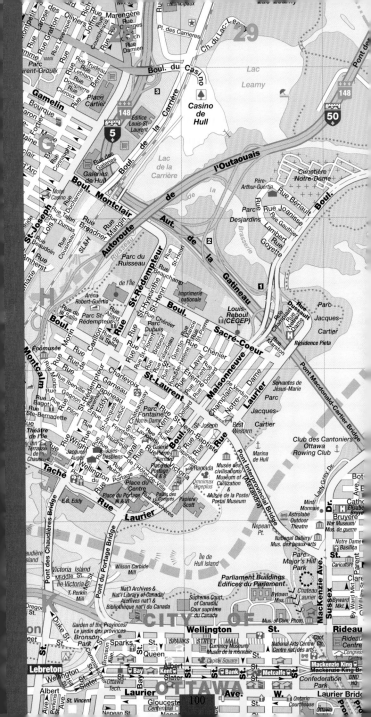

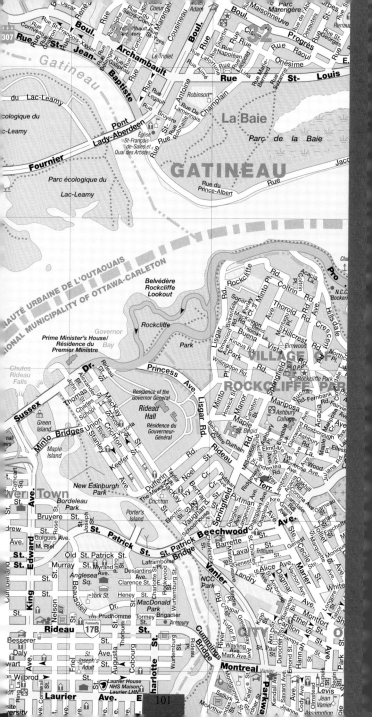

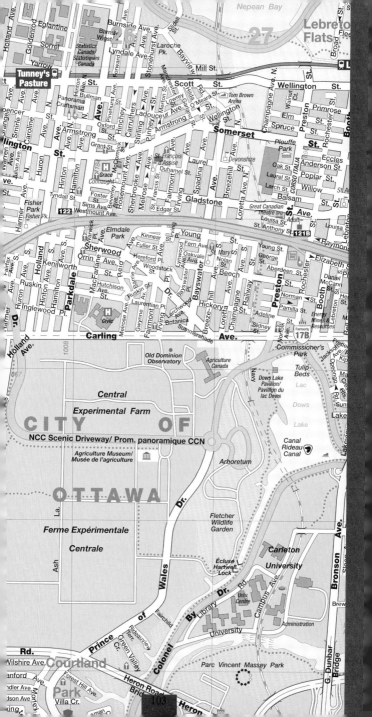

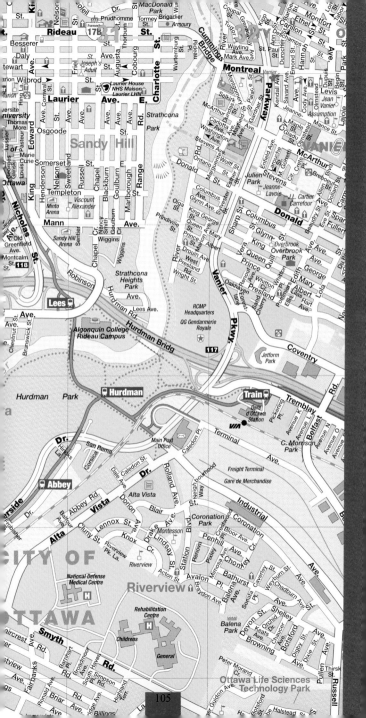

Map OTT 1: Pages 98, 99

Map OTT 3: Pages 102, 103

Map OTT 2: Pages 100, 101

Map OTT 4: Pages 104, 105

106

Glenview Ave. *OTT* 4 N29
Gloria Ave. *OTT* 4 P28
Gloucester St. *OTT* 4 L28-29
Glynn Ave. *OTT* 4 L31-32 M32
Golden Ave. *OTT* 3 L-M23
Goldenrod *OTT* 1 K25
Gordon St. *OTT* 4 N28
Goulburn Ave. *OTT* 4 L31
Goulburn Cr. *OTT* 4 L-M31
Gould St. *OTT* 3 L25
Graham Ave. *OTT* 4 M29-30
Grange Ave. *OTT* 3 L25
Grant St. *OTT* 3 L26
Granville Ave. *OTT* 3 L25
Green Valley Cr. *OTT* 3 O-P26
Greenbriar Ave. *OTT* 3 P25
Greenfield Ave. *OTT* 4 M30
Greenwood Ave. *OTT* 3 M23
Griffith Way *OTT* 3 P25
Grosvenor Ave. *OTT* 4 N-O28
Grove Ave. *OTT* 4 O28
Guertin Ave. *OTT* 4 P28
Guigues Ave. *OTT* 2 K30
Gwynne Ave. *OTT* 3 M26
Haig Dr. *OTT* 4 P32
Hall St. *OTT* 4 P32
Halstead St. *OTT* 4 P32
Hamilton Ave. N. 3 L25-26
Hamilton Ave. S. *OTT* 3 M25
Hamlet Rd. *OTT* 4 P32
Hampton Ave. *OTT* 3 L25
Harmer Ave. N. *OTT* 3 L-M25
Harmer Ave. S. *OTT* 3 M25
Harrold Pl. *OTT* 3 M25
Hart Ave. *OTT* 4 M32
Hartington Pl. *OTT* 4 L30
Harvard Ave. *OTT* 4 O28
Harvey St. *OTT* 4 M30
Hastings Ave. *OTT* 4 P32
Havelock St. *OTT* 4 M30
Hawthorne Ave. 4 M29-30
Hazel St. *OTT* 4 M29-30
Heath St. *OTT* 4 O30
Helena St. *OTT* 3 M25
Henderson Ave. *OTT* 4 L30
Hendricus *OTT* 3 M24
Heney St. *OTT* 2 K31
Henry St. *OTT* 3 M27
Hereford Pl. *OTT* 3 M26
Heron Rd. *OTT* 3 P26-27
Herridge St. *OTT* 4 N29-30
Hickory St. *OTT* 3 M26-27
Highcroft Ave. *OTT* 3 L23
Highland Ave. *OTT* 3 L-M23
Highland Terr. *OTT* 4 P31
Highridge Ave. *OTT* 4 P31
Hilda St. *OTT* 3 L26
Hill St. *OTT* 4 L28
Hillary Ave. *OTT* 4 P29
Hilson Ave. *OTT* 3 L-M24
Hinchey Ave. 1 K26 3 L26
Hincks La. *OTT* 4 N30
Hinton Ave. N. *OTT* 3 L25-26
Hinton Ave. S. *OTT* 3 M25
Hog's Back Rd. *OTT* 3 P26
Holland Ave. 1 K25-26 3 L-M25
Holmwood Ave. 4 N28-29

Hooper St. *OTT* 3 N24
Hopewell Ave. *OTT* 4 O28
Howick Pl. *OTT* 4 N29
Hudson Ave. *OTT* 3 P25
Hurdman Rd. *OTT* 4 M31
Huron Ave. N. *OTT* 3 L25
Huron Ave. S. *OTT* 3 M25
Hutchison Ave. *OTT* 3 M26
Hutton Ave. *OTT* 4 P32
Imperial Ave. *OTT* 4 M28
Industrial Ave. *OTT* 4 N-O32
Inglewood Pl. *OTT* 3 M25
Iona St. *OTT* 3 L24 L-M25
Irene Cr. *OTT* 3 M23
Irving Ave. *OTT* 3 L26
Irving Pl. *OTT* 3 M26
Isabella St. *OTT* 4 M29
Island Lodge Rd. *OTT* 2 K31
Island Park Cr. *OTT* 3 M24-25
Island Park Dr. 1 K24 3 L24 M24-25
Ivy Cr. *OTT* 2 J31-32
Jack Purcell La. *OTT* 4 L29
Jackson Ave. *OTT* 3 M27
James St. *OTT* 4 L28
Java St. *OTT* 3 L25
Jean-Jacques Lussier 4 L30
John St. *OTT* 2 J30-31
Julian Ave. *OTT* 3 L25
Junction Ave. *OTT* 4 P28
Keats Ave. *OTT* 4 O32
Keefer St. *OTT* 2 J31
Kenilworth St. *OTT* 3 M25-26
Kenora St. *OTT* 3 L25
Kensington Ave. *OTT* 3 L-M24
Kent St. *OTT* 4 L29
Kenwood Ave. *OTT* 3 L23
Kenzie St. *OTT* 3 N24
Kerr Ave. *OTT* 3 M23
Keyworth Ave. *OTT* 1 K25
Kilborn Ave. *OTT* 4 P29-30
Kilborn Pl. *OTT* 4 P29
King St. *OTT* 3 N24
King Edward Ave. 2 J-K30 4 L30
King George St. 4 L31-32 M32
Kings Ldg. *OTT* 4 M30
Kingston St. *OTT* 3 N-O24
Kinnear St. *OTT* 3 M26
Kintyre *OTT* 3 P25
Kippewa Dr. *OTT* 3 M27 4 M28
Kirchoffer Ave. *OTT* 1 K23 3 L23
Kirkwood Ave. *OTT* 3 L-N24
Knox Cr. *OTT* 4 O31
Laderoute Ave. *OTT* 3 L-M24
Ladouceur Ave. *OTT* 3 L26
Lady Ellen Pl. *OTT* 3 N23
Lady Grey Dr. *OTT* 2 J29-30
Laframboise Pl. *OTT* 2 K31
Lakeside Ave. 3 N27 4 N28
Lakeview Terr. 3 N27 4 N28
Lambton Ave. *OTT* 2 J32
Lamira St. *OTT* 4 P29
Lampman Cr. *OTT* 3 P26
Lanark Ave. *OTT* 1 K23-24
Langevin Ave. *OTT* 2 J-K32

Laperriere Ave. *OTT* 3 N23-24
Larch St. *OTT* 3 L27
Larchwood Ave. *OTT* 3 M26
Larkin St. *OTT* 3 N23-24
Larose Ave. *OTT* 3 N23-24
Lasalle St. *OTT* 4 P28
Latchford Rd. *OTT* 1 K24
Laurel St. *OTT* 3 L26-27
Laurentian Pl. *OTT* 3 M26
Laurier Ave. E. *OTT* 4 L30-31
Laurier Ave. W. *OTT* 4 L28-29
Leaside Ave. *OTT* 3 N24
Lebreton St. N. *OTT* 3 L-M27
Lebreton St. S. *OTT* 3 M27
Lees Ave. *OTT* 4 M30-31
Leighton Terr. *OTT* 3 L24
Lennox St. *OTT* 4 N-O31
Leonard Ave. *OTT* 4 O28
Lepage Ave. *OTT* 3 N23-24
Leslie Ave. *OTT* 4 O29
Letchworth Rd. *OTT* 4 N30
Lewis St. *OTT* 4 L29-30
Lexington St. *OTT* 3 P25
Library Rd. *OTT* 3 O26-27
Lilac La. *OTT* 4 P29
Lilas *OTT* 4 M32
Lincoln Ave. *OTT* 3 L23-24
Linden Terr. *OTT* 4 M29
Lindenlea Rd. *OTT* 2 J32
Lindsay St. *OTT* 4 O31
Lisgar St. *OTT* 4 L28-29
Livingstone Ave. *OTT* 4 P29
Lochaber Ave. *OTT* 3 L23
Logan Ave. *OTT* 4 O30
Lola St. *OTT* 4 N29-30
Loretta Ave. N. *OTT* 3 L-M27
Loretta Ave. S. *OTT* 3 M27
Lorne Ave. *OTT* 3 L27 4 L28
Louis Pasteur *OTT* 4 L30
Louisa St. *OTT* 3 L-M27
Lowrey St. *OTT* 3 L26
Lyman St. *OTT* 3 L24
Lynda La. *OTT* 4 P31
Lyndale Ave. *OTT* 1 K26
Lynwood Ave. *OTT* 3 M26
Lyon St. N. *OTT* 4 L-M28
Lyon St. S. *OTT* 4 M-N28
MacDonald St. *OTT* 4 L30
MacFarlane Ave. *OTT* 3 M26
MacKay St. *OTT* 2 J-K31
MacKenzie Ave. *OTT* 2 K29
MacLaren St. *OTT* 4 L28-29
MacLean St. *OTT* 3 M27 4 M28
Macy Blvd. *OTT* 3 M24
Madawaska Dr. 3 N27 4 N28
Madison Ave. *OTT* 3 L23
Mailes Ave. *OTT* 3 L24
Main St. *OTT* 4 N29-30
Malibu Terr. *OTT* 3 O-P25
Manchester Ave. 1 K26 3 L26
Mann Ave. *OTT* 4 L-M30
Maple La. *OTT* 2 J32
Marguerite Ave. *OTT* 4 L31-32
Marie Curie *OTT* 4 L30
Marion Ave. *OTT* 4 M31-32
Marlborough Ave. *OTT* 4 L31
Marlowe Cr. *OTT* 4 N30

INDEX

This index lists the main places, sights and hotels mentioned in this guide.

What do you get for your money?

Canada's loonie pales next to the powerful American dollar; however, Canadian prices are reasonable. Americans and other foreign visitors should convert their money into Canadian currency or traveller's cheques for convenience. Debit cards and credit cards are widely accepted. Let's go through an imaginary day in Ottawa (although this schedule is likely unrealistic time-wise) A cup of coffee will cost about $1: you'll pay more at gourmet coffee shops or hotel restaurants. Breakfast (two eggs, bacon, toast and coffee) will probably be under $5. Fill up your car with gasoline: Prices range from 60-cents to 75-cents a litre. A city tour on a double decker bus is $17.

A hamburger lunch will cost you between $5 and $12, depending whether you go for fast food or a roadhouse. Rent a bike for $7 an hour (or $20 for the day) at RentABike at the Chateau Laurier and head across the river to Hull to the Museum of Civilization. Admission is $8 (less at the other museums). Local phone calls are 25-cents. Postage is 46-cents for a letter mailed within Canada.

Can$	US$	UK
1	0.68	0.42
2	1.35	0.84
3	2.03	1.26
4	2.71	1.69
5	3.38	2.11
10	6.77	4.22
15	10.15	6.32
20	13.53	8.43
30	20.30	12.65
40	27.07	16.86
50	33.84	21.08
60	40.60	25.29
70	47.37	29.51
80	54.14	33.72
90	60.90	37.94
100	67.67	42.15
200	135.34	84.30
300	203.01	126.45
500	338.35	210.75
1000	676.70	421.50

Getting hungry again? A steak will cost about $15, sometimes more, depending on the restaurant. Get a bottle of domestic beer to go with it for just under $4. End your day with a movie: $8.50 to $10.

MARCO ● POLO

Discover Vancouver with Marco Polo
Canada's west coast offers plenty of natural beauty and cosmopolitan flair.

Marco Polo travel guides offer:
- Sightseeing highlights, walking tours
- Where to stay, dine and shop
- Compact size, maps, bright pictures
- Author's recommendations

Play the part of a tourist or blend like a local, but let Marco Polo be your guide.